POTENTIAL:

A GUIDE TO
Personal Mastery for Teenagers

Table of Contents

Introduction: A Journey to Mastery

1. Embracing Change

Understanding Change
   Quotes
The Importance of Embracing Change
   Think & Reflect
Change and Personal Growth
Change and Self-Discovery
Facing Fear of Change
Adapting to Change
Benefits of Adaptability
Adaptability in Animals
Change and Resilience
Change in Different Areas of Life
Embracing Change: A Step Towards Mastery
Case Studies of Embracing Change
Activities to Embrace Change
Embracing Change as a Teenager

2. Understanding Yourself

The Importance of Self-Understanding
Self-Identity
Personality
Values and Beliefs
Strengths and Weaknesses
Passions and Interests
Emotions and Feelings
Self-Reflection
Self-Awareness
Case Studies on Self-Understanding
Activities for Self-Understanding
The Journey to Self-Understanding

3. Setting Goals and Acting

The Importance of Goal Setting
Understanding Goals
Setting Personal Goals
Planning for Goals
Acting

Monitoring Progress
The Role of Self-Discipline in Goal Achievement
Case Studies on Goal Setting and Acting
Activities for Goal Setting and Acting
The Role of Support in Goal Achievement

4. Overcoming Challenges
Understanding Challenges
Facing Challenges
Problem-Solving Skills
   Further Reading
Resilience in Overcoming Challenges
Coping Strategies
The Role of Support in Overcoming Challenges
Case Studies on Overcoming Challenges
Activities for Overcoming Challenges
Challenges and Teenagers
Turning Challenges into Opportunities
Overcoming Challenges and Self-Confidence
Conclusion: The Power of Overcoming Challenges

5. Building Confidence and Self-Esteem
Understanding Confidence and Self-Esteem
   Further Reading
The Importance of Confidence and Self-Esteem
Building Confidence
Building Self-Esteem
Overcoming Confidence and Self-Esteem Challenges
The Role of Positive Self-Talk
Case Studies on Building Confidence and Self-Esteem
Activities for Building Confidence and Self-esteem
Confidence, Self-Esteem and Relationships
Confidence, Self-Esteem and Goal Achievement
The Power of Confidence and Self-Esteem

6. Developing Positive Habits
Understanding Habits
The Importance of Positive Habits
Creating Positive Habits
Overcoming Negative Habits
The Role of Willpower and Self-Discipline

Case Studies on Developing Positive Habits
Activities for Developing Positive Habits
Positive Habits and Self-Confidence
Positive Habits and Relationships
Positive Habits and Goal Achievement
Conclusion: The Power of Positive Habits

7. Managing Emotions and Stress

Understanding Emotions
Understanding Stress
Emotion Management
Stress Management
The Role of Mindfulness
Case Studies on Managing Emotions and Stress
Activities for Managing Emotions and Stress
Emotion and Stress Management and Self-confidence
    Further Reading
Emotion and Stress Management and Relationships
Emotion and Stress Management and Goal Achievement
The Power of Managing Emotions and Stress

8. Cultivating Resilience

Understanding Resilience
The Importance of Resilience
Building Resilience
Overcoming Resilience Challenges
The Role of Positive Mindset
Case Studies on Building Resilience
Activities for Building Resilience
    Further Reading
Resilience and Self-Confidence
Resilience and Relationships
Resilience and Goal Achievement
The Power of Resilience

9. Nurturing Relationships

Understanding Relationships
The Importance of Healthy Relationships
Building Healthy Relationships
Overcoming Relationship Challenges
The Role of Communication

Case Studies on Nurturing Relationships
Activities for Nurturing Relationships
Relationships and Self-Confidence
    Further Reading
Relationships and Goal Achievement
The Power of Nurturing Relationships

10. Communicating Effectively
Understanding Communication
The Importance of Effective Communication
Communication and Personal Growth
Improving Communication Skills
Building Effective Communication Skills
Overcoming Communication Challenges
The Role of Listening
Case Studies on Effective Communication
Activities for Building Effective Communication Skills
Effective Communication and Self-confidence
    Famous Quotes
Effective Communication and Goal Achievement
Conclusion: The Power of Effective Communication

11. Time Management and Productivity
Understanding Time Management
The Importance of Time Management
Building Time Management Skills
Overcoming Time Management Challenges
Understanding Productivity
Case Studies on Time Management and Productivity
Activities for Building Time Management Skills
Time Management, Productivity and Self-confidence
    Test Your Knowledge
Time Management, Productivity and Goal Achievement
The Power of Time Management and Productivity

12. Exploring Passions and Interests
Understanding Passions and Interests
The Importance of Exploring Passions and Interests
Discovering Your Passions and Interests
Overcoming Challenges in Exploring Passions and Interests
Challenges in Pursuing Passions and Interests

Support Systems and Their Impact
The Role of Passions and Interests in Career Choices
Case Studies on Exploring Passions and Interests
Activities for Exploring Passions and Interests
  Further Reading
Passions, Interests and Self-Confidence
Passions, Interests and Goal Achievement
The Power of Exploring Passions and Interests

13. Mindfulness and Self-awareness
Understanding Mindfulness
The Importance of Mindfulness
Practicing Mindfulness
Understanding Self-Awareness
The Importance of Self-Awareness
Jon Kabat-Zinn: A Pioneer in Mindfulness
Building Self-Awareness
Overcoming Challenges in Mindfulness and Self-Awareness
Case Studies on Mindfulness and Self-awareness
Activities for Building Mindfulness and Self-awareness
Mindfulness, Self-Awareness and Self-confidence

14. Finding Balance in Life
Understanding Life Balance
The Importance of Life Balance
Achieving Life Balance
Overcoming Challenges in Achieving Life Balance
The Role of Life Balance in Stress Management
Case Studies on Life Balance
Activities for Achieving Life Balance
Life Balance and Self-Confidence
Life Balance and Goal Achievement
  Famous Quotes
The Power of Life Balance

15. Making Decisions and Taking Ownership
Understanding Decision Making
The Importance of Decision Making
Effective Decision Making
Understanding Ownership
The Importance of Taking Ownership

    Think & Reflect
Taking Ownership Effectively
Overcoming Challenges in Decision Making and Taking Ownership
Case Studies on Decision Making and Taking Ownership
Activities for Decision Making and Taking Ownership
    Famous Quotes
Decision Making, Ownership and Self-confidence
The Power of Decision Making and Taking Ownership

16. Adapting to Change
The Importance of Adapting to Change
Effective Adaptation to Change
Overcoming Challenges in Adapting to Change
The Role of Change in Stress Management
Case Studies on Adapting to Change
Activities for Adapting to Change
    Think & Reflect
Adapting to Change and Self-Confidence
Adapting to Change and Goal Achievement
The Power of Adapting to Change

17. Building a Support System
Understanding a Support System
The Importance of a Support System
Building an Effective Support System
Overcoming Challenges in Building a Support System
    Further Reading
The Role of a Support System in Stress Management
    Think & Reflect
Case Studies on Building a Support System
Activities for Building a Support System
Support System and Self-Confidence
Support System and Goal Achievement
The Power of a Support System

18. Respecting Yourself and Others
Understanding Respect
    Further Reading
The Importance of Self-Respect
Cultivating Self-Respect
The Importance of Respecting Others
Cultivating Respect for Others

Overcoming Challenges in Respecting Yourself and Others
Case Studies on Respecting Yourself and Others
Activities for Respecting Yourself and Others
Respect, Self-Confidence and Self-Esteem
The Power of Respecting Yourself and Others

19. Celebrating Growth and Progress

Understanding Growth and Progress
The Importance of Celebrating Growth and Progress
Ways to Celebrate Growth and Progress
Overcoming Challenges in Celebrating Growth and Progress
The Role of Celebration in Stress Management
Case Studies on Celebrating Growth and Progress
Activities for Celebrating Growth and Progress
Celebration and Self-Confidence
Celebration and Goal Achievement
   Further Reading
Conclusion: The Power of Celebrating Growth and Progress

20. Looking Ahead: Your Journey to Mastery

Understanding Mastery
The Journey to Mastery
Setting Goals for Mastery
Overcoming Challenges in the Journey to Mastery
The Role of a Support System in the Journey to Mastery
Thomas Edison: A Master of Invention
Case Studies on the Journey to Mastery
Activities for the Journey to Mastery
Mastery and Self-Confidence
Mastery and Goal Achievement
The Power of Mastery

INTRODUCTION: A JOURNEY TO MASTERY

This book, "Potential: A Guide to Personal Mastery for Teenagers," is dedicated to my daughters, Olivia and Talia. Being a father to these incredible young women is the most significant role I have ever undertaken, and they have been my source of joy and inspiration since the first moment when Talia made me a Daddy sixteen years ago.

As I write this, Olivia who is thirteen and Talia who is sixteen have found mastery in their own arenas, leading to self-confidence, positive self-images, and fulfilling interactions with friends, boys, parents, and teachers alike. They attract like-minded friends and bring positivity into their lives because they know what they want and what they like.

Olivia and Talia, you are the reason for this book. It is my hope that this guide will help you and other teenagers like you to master the things that bring the most joy. This book isn't about simply finding your passion; it's about understanding that life isn't always fair and that challenges are inevitable. It's about creating a framework for navigating those challenges and using them to propel yourselves forward.

Life can either spiral up or down, and this book is designed to help you embrace the upward spiral. It's about understanding change, dealing with it head-on, and honing the skills needed to navigate it. As you grow, your bodies, friends, and interests will change. This guide will help you handle those changes, set goals, and take action to achieve them.

Understand that overcoming challenges is not just a platitude; it's a muscle you can strengthen. Self-esteem is not handed to you; it is earned through hard work and dedication. The habits you develop as teenagers will carry you through life, both good and bad. This book will teach you how to manage stress and emotions, cultivate resilience, communicate effectively, manage your time, and explore your interests and potential passions.

Being mindful, breathing, and becoming self-aware are essential. Knowing when to behave a certain way and recognizing when those around you lack these tools will help you navigate and leave difficult situations. Balance is crucial knowing when to step back and play, embracing people from all walks of life, and giving them the space to be themselves.

This guide also emphasizes the importance of making decisions independently, respecting yourself, your body, your reputation, and the reputation of your family, friends, community, and country. Offer respect to all and fear nobody. Celebrate your wins, growth, and progress along the way, and embrace the journey to mastery because that's what it is—a journey, not a destination.

Olivia, you shine in school and excel in athletics, advocating for your right to participate in the sports you love. Talia, you have discovered your potential in theater and thrive as a phenomenal student, singer and performer. You both have forged your paths and continue to fulfill your limitless potential. These lessons I have shared with you, I now wish to share with the world.

Special moments like our dinner tradition, where we share compliments around the table, and our morning ritual where I say, "Have a great day...and?" and you reply, "Make it a great day for somebody else," are dear to my heart. Also, when I ask, "Who is your number one?" you always reply, "Each other," knowing that when your mom and I are long gone, you will always have each other.

This book is my gift to you and to every teenager seeking to master their potential. I love you, Olivia and Talia, and

I am incredibly proud of you. Keep up the good work.

1. EMBRACING CHANGE

Understanding Change

Change is a constant in the universe, an inevitable process that signifies the transition from one state to another. It is the movement through time and experiences that transforms environments, situations, and individuals. Change can be as simple as a new hairstyle or as complex as a shift in cultural norms. It is the progression of life's moments, both significant and trivial, that collectively shape the world around us.

In the context of personal development, change is the evolution of one's thoughts, behaviors, and emotions. It is the journey from who you are to who you are becoming. Embracing change is essential for growth and learning, as it challenges us to adapt and expand our perspectives.

Types of Change

Change manifests in various forms, each with its own set of characteristics and impacts. Physical change involves alterations in the material world, such as the changing of seasons or the construction of a new building. Emotional change refers to shifts in feelings and moods, like the joy of making a new friend or the sadness of a loss. Intellectual change is the expansion of knowledge and understanding, which can occur through education or personal experiences.

Social change encompasses the transformation of relationships and societal structures, while psychological change is the internal development of attitudes and mental processes. Recognizing these types of change helps us understand how they influence our lives and the world around us.

When you approach the world around you as something that is in constant flux, and change, you won't be caught off guard when life throws change your way. This sounds easy. It's not. Being prepared for change is the first step toward your growth out of childhood and into adulthood.

The Role of Change in Life

Change plays a pivotal role in life, serving as a driving force for progress and innovation. It challenges the status quo, pushing individuals and societies to evolve and improve. Change can be a source of inspiration, prompting new ideas and creative solutions to problems. It also tests our adaptability and resilience, teaching us valuable lessons about ourselves and the world.

In personal terms, change is often the catalyst for self-improvement. It encourages us to reflect on our lives, reassess our goals, and strive for a better future. Without change, there would be no growth, no learning, and no advancement. It is an essential component of the human experience.

Quotes

"The only way to make sense out of change is to plunge into it, move with it, and join the dance." - Alan Watts

Alan Watts, a British philosopher, writer, and speaker, encourages us to embrace change and see it as a dance. Instead of resisting it, we should move with it and enjoy the rhythm of life.

"Change is the law of life. And those who look only to the past or present are certain to miss the future." - John F. Kennedy

John F. Kennedy, the 35th President of the United States, reminds us that change is inevitable. By focusing only on the past or present, we risk missing out on the opportunities that the future may bring.

"It is not the strongest of the species that survive, nor the most intelligent, but the one most responsive to change." - Charles Darwin

Charles Darwin, the father of evolution, emphasizes the importance of adaptability. The ability to respond to change is a key factor in survival and success.

"Change your life today. Don't gamble on the future, act now, without delay." - Simone de Beauvoir

Simone de Beauvoir, a French writer and philosopher, urges us to take action now. Change is not something to be left to chance; it requires deliberate action and commitment.

The Importance of Embracing Change

Benefits of Embracing Change

Embracing change has numerous benefits. It opens doors to new opportunities and experiences that can enrich our lives. When we welcome change, we cultivate a mindset of flexibility and openness, which is crucial for personal and professional success. Embracing change also fosters creativity, as it requires us to think outside the box and find innovative solutions to challenges.

Additionally, accepting change can lead to improved relationships. By understanding that people and circumstances evolve, we can maintain stronger, more adaptable connections with others. Embracing change also contributes to our overall well-being, as it encourages a proactive approach to life, rather than a reactive one.

Consequences of Resisting Change

Resisting change can have negative consequences. It can lead to stagnation, where personal growth is hindered, and opportunities are missed. Resistance to change can also cause stress and anxiety, as the inevitable shifts in life become sources of fear rather than moments for development. This resistance can strain relationships, as an inability to adapt to the changes in others can create conflict and misunderstanding.

Furthermore, resisting change can limit one's potential. By clinging to the familiar, individuals may fail to discover new passions, skills, and aspects of their identity. It is important to recognize that while change can be uncomfortable, the consequences of resisting it are often more detrimental than the change itself.

Let me end with this. If you can't embrace change, you'll stagnate. If you stagnate you will be surpassed by others. If you're surpassed by others you will lose out on opporutnities that are presented to you.

For example: You may be used to playing a certain role on a team or school club you're a member of. Perhaps the coach decides to move you to another position. If you're upset by this, you may get benched. If you accept that change is the norm, and that this change could potentially be a good thing. You can move to the new position with a new found focus and joy. Opening doors you never thought were there.

Retired Football player, Jason Kelce used to play linebacker in high school. When he got to college his coaches decided to move him to center. He didn't want to make that change, but because he was comfortable with change, he embraced his new role, and is a future Hall of Famer.

Think & Reflect

Change is a constant part of life, and how we react to it can greatly impact our personal growth and happiness. Consider the following questions to better understand your relationship with change:

1. Can you recall a time when you resisted change? What were the consequences?

2. How did you feel during that time? Did you experience any of the negative effects mentioned in the text, such as stress, anxiety, or conflict?

3. Now, think of a time when you embraced change. How did that experience differ from the time you resisted change?

4. What new opportunities, skills, or aspects of your identity were you able to discover as a result of embracing change?

5. How can you apply these reflections to future changes in your life?

Remember, embracing change doesn't mean you have to like every change that comes your way. It means recognizing that change is inevitable and using it as an opportunity for growth and self-discovery.

There's no room for temper tantrums in the real world. The sooner you realize this, the happier you'll be.

Change and Personal Growth

How Change Leads to Growth

Change is a powerful agent of personal growth. It challenges us to leave our comfort zones and face new situations, which can lead to the development of new skills and knowledge. Through change, we learn to adapt, problem-solve, and persevere, all of which are essential qualities for personal mastery.

Growth through change is not always easy or comfortable, but it is through overcoming these challenges that we build character and resilience. Each change we encounter is an opportunity to learn more about ourselves, to test our limits, and to expand our capabilities.

Examples of Personal Growth Through Change

Personal growth through change can be seen in various scenarios. A teenager who moves to a new city may initially struggle with the transition but eventually makes new friends and discovers new interests. Another example is a student who takes on a challenging course and, through hard work and determination, gains a deeper understanding of the subject and a sense of accomplishment.

These experiences demonstrate that while change can be daunting, it is also an opportunity for significant personal development. By embracing change, individuals can transform challenges into stepping stones for growth.

Change and Self-Discovery

Exploring New Aspects of Self

Change encourages self-discovery by pushing individuals to explore new aspects of their identity. When faced with new situations, people are often required to tap into parts of themselves that they may not have been aware of before. This exploration can lead to the discovery of hidden talents, interests, and values.

For example, a teenager who volunteers for a community service project may discover a passion for helping others, which could shape their future career choices and personal goals. Change provides the context for such self-exploration, which is a critical component of personal mastery.

Change as a Catalyst for Self-Discovery

Change acts as a catalyst for self-discovery by creating situations that require introspection and self-assessment. It prompts individuals to question their beliefs, goals, and desires, leading to a deeper understanding of who they are and what they want from life.

This process of self-discovery is essential for personal growth and fulfillment. By embracing change and the self-exploration it brings, individuals can align their lives with their true selves, leading to a more authentic and satisfying existence.

Facing Fear of Change

Understanding Fear of Change

Fear of change is a common experience, rooted in the uncertainty and unpredictability that change brings. It is a natural response to the potential risks and losses associated with leaving the familiar behind. This fear can manifest as anxiety, reluctance, or even outright refusal to engage with new experiences.

Understanding this fear is the first step in overcoming it. Recognizing that it is a normal reaction allows individuals to address it constructively, rather than allowing it to hinder their growth and opportunities.

Strategies to Overcome Fear of Change

Overcoming the fear of change involves several strategies. One effective approach is to focus on the potential benefits of change, rather than the risks. This positive framing can help shift one's mindset from fear to anticipation.

Another strategy is to take small steps towards embracing change. Gradual exposure to new experiences can make the process less intimidating and more manageable. Additionally, seeking support from friends, family, or mentors can provide encouragement and guidance through the transition.

Adapting to Change

Skills Needed to Adapt to Change

Adapting to change requires a set of skills that enable individuals to navigate new circumstances effectively. These skills include flexibility, the ability to think critically, and the willingness to learn. Being flexible allows one to adjust to changing situations without excessive stress. Critical thinking helps in assessing new information and making informed decisions. A willingness to learn ensures that individuals remain open to new knowledge and experiences.

Other important skills include emotional intelligence, which aids in managing one's emotions during times of change, and problem-solving, which is crucial for overcoming obstacles that may arise.

Practicing Adaptability

Practicing adaptability involves putting oneself in situations that require flexibility and openness to change. This could mean trying new activities, taking on different roles, or simply changing up daily routines. By regularly stepping out of one's comfort zone, individuals can build their adaptability muscles, making it easier to handle larger changes when they occur.

It is also helpful to reflect on past experiences with change, identifying what strategies worked and what could be improved. This reflection can inform future approaches to change, making the process of adaptation more efficient and effective.

Benefits of Adaptability

Problem-solving: Adaptable people can think creatively and come up with new solutions to problems.

Resilience: Those who are adaptable are better equipped to deal with life's ups and downs, making them more resilient in the face of adversity.

Learning: Adaptability promotes a growth mindset, which can lead to continuous learning and personal development.

Adaptability in Animals

Did you know that adaptability is also a key survival trait in the animal kingdom? For example, the Arctic fox changes its fur color with the seasons to blend in with its environment, and the chameleon can change its color to communicate or hide from predators.

Change and Resilience

Building Resilience Through Change

Resilience is the ability to bounce back from adversity and is closely linked to one's capacity to handle change. Building resilience involves facing challenges and learning from them, rather than avoiding them. Each time an individual successfully navigates a change, their resilience is strengthened.

Resilience is not an innate trait but a skill that can be developed over time. It requires a positive attitude, the ability to manage stress, and a strong support network. By cultivating these elements, individuals can enhance their resilience and their ability to thrive in the face of change.

Examples of Resilience in the Face of Change

Examples of resilience in the face of change can be found in various contexts. A student who fails a test but studies harder and improves their grades demonstrates resilience. Similarly, a teenager who experiences a painful breakup but learns from the experience and forms healthier relationships in the future is showing resilience.

These examples illustrate that resilience is not about never facing difficulties, but about growing from them. It is a key component of successfully embracing change and achieving personal mastery.

Change in Different Areas of Life

Change in Personal Relationships

Change in personal relationships is inevitable as individuals grow and evolve. Friendships may shift as interests diverge, and family dynamics can change as members go through different life stages. Navigating these changes requires communication, empathy, and a willingness to adapt to new relationship dynamics.

Embracing change in relationships can lead to deeper connections and a better understanding of oneself and others. It is an opportunity to learn how to relate to a diverse range of people and to appreciate the unique contributions each person brings to one's life.

Change in School and Learning

Change in school and learning is a constant part of the educational journey. Students encounter new subjects, teachers, and learning environments as they progress through their education. These changes can be challenging but also offer chances to discover new passions and strengths.

Adapting to change in the academic realm fosters intellectual growth and prepares students for the ever-evolving nature of the workforce and society. It teaches them to be lifelong learners, always ready to acquire new knowledge and skills.

Change in Personal Interests and Passions

As teenagers explore different aspects of their identity, their personal interests and passions may change. This is a natural part of self-discovery and should be embraced. Pursuing new hobbies or activities can lead to unexpected joys and a more well-rounded sense of self.

Change in interests also encourages versatility and adaptability, qualities that are highly valuable in all areas of life. It allows individuals to experience the richness of life's offerings and to find fulfillment in a variety of pursuits.

Embracing Change: A Step Towards Mastery

How Embracing Change Contributes to Mastery

Embracing change is a critical step towards personal mastery. Mastery involves a deep understanding and command of various aspects of life, including one's emotions, behaviors, and thoughts. By welcoming change, individuals demonstrate a commitment to continuous improvement and learning.

The process of embracing change develops the skills and attitudes necessary for mastery, such as resilience, adaptability, and self-awareness. It is through the challenges and opportunities that change presents that individuals can truly refine their abilities and move towards mastery.

The Journey to Mastery: An Ongoing Process

The journey to mastery is an ongoing process that does not have a definitive end. It is a lifelong pursuit of growth, learning, and self-improvement. Embracing change is a fundamental part of this journey, as it propels individuals forward and prevents complacency.

Mastery is not about achieving perfection but about striving for excellence and being open to the lessons that change brings. It is about continually evolving and adapting, always seeking to better oneself and one's circumstances.

Case Studies of Embracing Change

Real-Life Examples of Embracing Change

There are countless real-life examples of individuals who have embraced change and achieved personal mastery. These stories can serve as inspiration and guidance for those on their own journey. Case studies may include famous figures who overcame adversity, as well as everyday people who made significant life changes to pursue their dreams.

These examples highlight the transformative power of change and the potential it holds for personal growth and fulfillment. They show that with the right mindset and approach, change can be a positive and rewarding experience.

Lessons Learned from Case Studies

The lessons learned from case studies of embracing change are varied and valuable. They teach us that change is not something to be feared but to be welcomed as an opportunity for growth. They demonstrate the importance of resilience, adaptability, and a positive outlook.

These case studies also show that support from others can be instrumental in navigating change. They remind us that everyone's journey is unique and that there is no one-size-fits-all approach to embracing change.

Activities to Embrace Change

Practical Exercises to Embrace Change

Practical exercises to embrace change can help individuals develop the skills and mindset needed to navigate life's transitions. These exercises might include goal-setting activities, role-playing scenarios, or journaling prompts that encourage reflection on past changes and future aspirations.

Engaging in these activities can build confidence and provide a framework for handling change more effectively. They can also be a source of motivation and inspiration, helping individuals to see the possibilities that change brings.

Reflective Activities on Change

Reflective activities on change are designed to deepen one's understanding of the role change plays in their life. These might include meditation, guided visualization, or discussions with peers about experiences with change. Reflecting on change helps individuals process their feelings and thoughts about it, leading to greater acceptance and readiness to embrace it.

These reflective practices can also provide clarity and insight, helping individuals to align their actions with their goals and values. They are an important part of the journey to embracing change and achieving personal mastery.

Embracing Change as a Teenager

The Unique Challenges and Opportunities of Change for Teenagers

Teenagers face unique challenges and opportunities when it comes to change. This period of life is marked by rapid development and significant transitions, such as moving from middle school to high school or preparing for college. These changes can be overwhelming, but they also offer a chance for teenagers to shape their identities and futures.

By embracing change, teenagers can take control of their personal growth and set the foundation for a fulfilling life. They can learn valuable skills that will serve them well into adulthood and discover what truly matters to them.

Looking Forward: Embracing Change in the Journey to Mastery

Looking forward, embracing change is an essential part of the journey to personal mastery. It is a skill that will be called upon time and again throughout life. For teenagers, learning to embrace change now can set the stage for a lifetime of growth, achievement, and personal fulfillment.

As they continue on their path to mastery, teenagers will find that their experiences with change have prepared them to face the future with confidence and resilience. Embracing change is not just about adapting to the new; it is about actively shaping one's destiny and becoming the best version of oneself.

◆ ◆ ◆

1. What is one of the benefits of embracing change?

    A. It keeps your life predictable and comfortable.
    B. It prevents you from facing challenges.
    C. It leads to personal growth.
    D. It allows you to avoid new experiences.

2. How does change contribute to self-discovery?

    A. It keeps you in your comfort zone.
    B. It ensures that your life remains the same.
    C. It allows you to explore new aspects of yourself.
    D. It prevents you from making mistakes.

3. What is one strategy to overcome fear of change?

    A. Avoiding situations that require change.
    B. Resisting change at all costs.
    C. Sticking to familiar routines and habits.
    D. Practicing adaptability.

4. How does embracing change contribute to mastery?

    A. It keeps you stuck in the past.
    B. It is an ongoing process that leads to personal growth and selfimprovement.
    C. It ensures that you never face any challenges.
    D. It prevents you from learning new skills.

2. UNDERSTANDING YOURSELF

The Importance of Self-Understanding

1.1. Benefits of Self-Understanding

Self-understanding is the foundation of personal growth and mastery. When you understand who you are, you can make more informed decisions, set goals that align with your true self, and pursue a life that brings you joy and fulfillment. Knowing your strengths and weaknesses allows you to leverage your abilities and work on areas that need improvement. Self-understanding also enhances your relationships with others, as it fosters empathy and better communication.

1.2. Self-Understanding and Personal Mastery

Personal mastery is about taking control of your life's direction and living with purpose. It requires a deep understanding of your inner world—your thoughts, feelings, motivations, and desires. With self-understanding, you can steer your life towards your vision of success, overcome obstacles with greater resilience, and live authentically. It's a critical step in becoming the best version of yourself.

Self-Identity

2.1. What is Self-Identity?

Self-identity is your sense of who you are as an individual. It's the internal narrative that includes your personal history, your beliefs about yourself, and how you see your place in the world. This narrative is shaped by your experiences, culture, and the people around you. It's important to recognize that self-identity is not static; it evolves as you grow and learn more about yourself.

2.2. Components of Self-Identity

Your self-identity is composed of various elements, including your personal values, the roles you play in life, your relationships, and your aspirations. It also includes your self-image, which is how you perceive your physical and personal attributes. Understanding these components helps you to see the multifaceted nature of your identity and appreciate the complexity of who you are.

2.3. Developing a Healthy Self-Identity

Developing a healthy self-identity involves self-acceptance and self-compassion. It means recognizing your inherent worth, embracing your uniqueness, and acknowledging that you are more than your mistakes or achievements. A healthy self-identity provides a stable foundation for personal growth and helps you navigate life's challenges with confidence.

Personality

3.1. Understanding Personality

Personality refers to the unique patterns of thoughts, feelings, and behaviors that make you who you are. It's influenced by both genetic factors and life experiences. Understanding your personality can help you recognize why you react to certain situations in specific ways and how you relate to others.

3.2. Personality Traits

Personality traits are the consistent patterns in the way you behave, think, and feel. For example, you might be naturally outgoing or introverted, organized or spontaneous. These traits can be assessed through various frameworks, such as the Big Five personality traits, which include openness, conscientiousness, extraversion, agreeableness, and neuroticism.

3.3. How Personality Influences Behavior

Your personality has a significant impact on your behavior and the choices you make in life. For instance, if you're highly conscientious, you might be more inclined to plan ahead and strive for high achievement. Understanding the influence of your personality can help you make choices that align with your natural tendencies and lead to greater satisfaction.

Values and Beliefs

4.1. Identifying Your Values

Values are the principles that guide your behavior and decision-making. They reflect what is important to you and what you stand for. Identifying your values involves reflecting on moments when you felt fulfilled or proud, as well as times when you were disappointed or upset. These reflections can reveal the underlying values that drive your actions.

4.2. Understanding Your Beliefs

Beliefs are the convictions you hold to be true, often without the need for immediate proof. They can be about yourself, others, or the world in general. Your beliefs shape your perception of reality and can either empower you or hold you back. It's important to examine your beliefs critically and determine whether they serve your growth or need reevaluation.

4.3. How Values and Beliefs Influence Decisions

Your values and beliefs are like an internal compass that directs your life's path. They influence the goals you set, the relationships you pursue, and the way you respond to challenges. When your decisions are aligned with your values and beliefs, you're more likely to feel a sense of integrity and satisfaction with your life choices.

Strengths and Weaknesses

5.1. Identifying Your Strengths

Identifying your strengths involves recognizing the things you excel at or the qualities that come naturally to you. These could be skills like communication or creativity, or character strengths such as kindness or resilience. Knowing your strengths allows you to leverage them in various aspects of your life, from school to personal relationships.

5.2. Understanding Your Weaknesses

Understanding your weaknesses is not about dwelling on your shortcomings, but rather about acknowledging areas where you can improve. It's an opportunity for growth and learning. When you're aware of your weaknesses, you can seek support, develop new skills, and make choices that minimize their impact on your life.

5.3. Leveraging Strengths and Addressing Weaknesses

Leveraging your strengths means using them to your

advantage in achieving your goals and overcoming obstacles. Addressing your weaknesses involves setting personal development goals and taking steps to improve or compensate for them. Balancing the two can lead to a more fulfilling and successful life.

Passions and Interests

6.1. Discovering Your Passions

Passions are the activities or subjects that deeply excite and energize you.
Discovering your passions may require exploration and experimentation. It's about paying attention to what activities make you lose track of time and what topics you're naturally drawn to learn more about.

6.2. Exploring Your Interests

Interests are the curiosities that you have about the world. They can be related to your passions or entirely separate. Exploring your interests involves trying new things, asking questions, and engaging with diverse experiences. This exploration can lead to a richer, more varied life.

6.3. How Passions and Interests Contribute to Self-Understanding

Your passions and interests provide insight into what motivates and fulfills you. They can reveal your values and the type of life you aspire to live. Engaging with your passions and interests can also boost your self-esteem and provide a sense of purpose.

Emotions and Feelings

7.1. Understanding Your Emotions

Emotions are complex responses to internal or external events. Understanding your emotions involves recognizing what you feel, identifying the triggers, and acknowledging the impact of these emotions on your behavior. Emotional intelligence is the ability to understand and manage your emotions effectively.

7.2. Managing Your Feelings

Managing your feelings doesn't mean suppressing them; it means expressing them in healthy and appropriate ways. It involves developing coping strategies, such as mindfulness or talking to someone you trust, to deal with challenging emotions. It also means cultivating positive emotions to enhance your well-being.

7.3. Emotions as a Tool for Self-Understanding

Your emotions can serve as a tool for self-understanding by providing clues about your needs and values. They can signal when something is wrong, when you need to set boundaries, or when you're aligned with your true self. By paying attention to your emotions, you can gain deeper insights into who you are.

Self-Reflection

8.1. The Role of Self-Reflection in Self-Understanding

Self-reflection is the practice of thoughtfully considering your own behaviors, beliefs, and motivations. It plays a crucial role in self-understanding by helping you to process experiences, recognize patterns, and make conscious changes. Reflecting on your actions and decisions leads to greater self-awareness and personal growth.

8.2. Practicing Self-Reflection

Practicing self-reflection can be done through journaling, meditation, or simply taking time to think deeply about your day. It's important to approach self-reflection with an open mind and a willingness to learn about yourself. Regular self-reflection can lead to profound insights and transformative change.

8.3. Benefits of Regular Self-Reflection

Engaging in regular self-reflection can improve your decision-making, increase your emotional intelligence, and enhance your relationships. It allows you to live more intentionally and align your actions with your core values. The benefits of self-reflection extend to all areas of your life, contributing to a more meaningful and authentic existence.

Self-Awareness

9.1. What is Self-Awareness?

Self-awareness is the conscious knowledge of your own character, feelings, motives, and desires. It's the ability to see yourself clearly and objectively through reflection and introspection. Being self-aware allows you to understand how others perceive you and how you fit into the larger world.

9.2. Developing Self-Awareness

Developing self-awareness is a continuous process that involves seeking feedback, observing your thoughts and behaviors, and challenging your assumptions. It requires curiosity about your inner world and the courage to face what you discover. As you develop self-awareness, you gain the power to change aspects of yourself and your life.

9.3. The Role of Self-Awareness in Self-Understanding

Self-awareness is a key component of self-understanding. It enables you to recognize your patterns, both positive and negative, and to make informed choices about how to act and react in various situations. With self-awareness, you can navigate life with greater confidence and authenticity.

Case Studies on Self-Understanding

10.1. Real-Life Examples of Self-Understanding

Case studies of individuals who have achieved a high level of self-understanding can be inspiring and instructive. These stories often highlight the journey of self-discovery, the challenges faced, and the strategies used to overcome them. They show the transformative power of self-understanding in action.

10.2. Lessons Learned from Case Studies

From these case studies, we can learn valuable lessons about the importance of self-reflection, the courage to face one's fears, and the benefits of embracing one's true self. They teach us that self-understanding is not a destination but a lifelong journey that requires continuous effort and commitment.

Activities for Self-Understanding

11.1. Practical Exercises for Self-Understanding

There are many practical exercises that can help you on your journey to self-understanding. These might include personality tests, journaling prompts, or guided meditations focused on self-discovery. Engaging in these activities can provide clarity and insight into your inner world.

11.2. Reflective Activities for Self-Understanding

Reflective activities, such as writing a personal mission statement or creating a vision board, can help you articulate your values, goals, and aspirations. They encourage you to think deeply about what you want from life and how you can achieve it.

Answer these questions to create your own personal mission statement:

1. **Self-Reflection:**
     - What activities or subjects are you most passionate about?
     - What values are most important to you (e.g., honesty, creativity, helping others)?
     - What strengths and skills do you possess that make you unique?

2. **Vision and Goals:**
     - What are your long-term goals or dreams for the future?
     - How do you want to impact the world or your community?
     - Where do you see yourself in five or ten years?

3. **Purpose and Motivation:**
     - Why do you get up in the morning? What motivates you?
     - Who or what inspires you the most? Why?
     - What do you want to be remembered for?

4. **Interests and Hobbies:**
    - What activities do you enjoy doing in your free time?
    - What hobbies or interests would you like to develop further?
    - Are there any causes or issues you feel strongly about?

5. **Contribution and Legacy:**
    - How do you want to contribute to your family, school, or community?
    - What difference do you want to make in the lives of others?
    - What legacy do you want to leave behind?

Process:

1. **Gather Responses:** Write down your answers to the questions above.

2. **Identify Themes:** Look for common themes or recurring ideas in your responses.

3. **Draft the Statement:** Create a draft mission statement that combines your values, goals, and motivations.

4. **Refine and Review:** Review the draft together with your friends and family, making adjustments to ensure it truly reflects your aspirations and values.

5. **Finalize:** Make sure it's clear, concise, and inspiring

to you!

Example Mission Statement from the Author, Chris Dessi

"To use my creativity and passion for writing and coaching to solve real-world problems, inspire others through innovative projects, and contribute to a more connected and compassionate world."

The Journey to Self-Understanding

12.1. The Ongoing Process of Self-Understanding

Self-understanding is not a one-time event but an ongoing process that evolves as you grow and change. It requires patience, self-compassion, and a commitment to personal development. As you continue this journey, you'll find that self-understanding enriches every aspect of your life.

12.2. Looking Forward: Self-Understanding in the Journey to Mastery

As you look forward, remember that self-understanding is a vital step in the journey to personal mastery. It empowers you to live with purpose, make meaningful choices, and pursue your true potential. Embrace the journey of self-discovery, for it is the path to a fulfilling and authentic life.

1. What is the primary benefit of self-understanding?

    A. It helps you make better decisions
    B. It makes you more popular
    C. It increases your height
    D. It improves your grades

2. What is a component of self-identity?

    A. Your personality traits

    B. Your favorite food
    C. Your favorite color
    D. Your favorite movie

3. How do values and beliefs influence decisions?

    A hey determine what you consider right or wrong
    B. They determine your favorite color

C. They have no influence on decisions
D. They influence your physical appearance

4. What is the role of self-reflection in self-understanding?

   A. It helps you understand your favorite movie
   B. It helps you understand your favorite color
   C. It helps you understand your favorite food
   D. It helps you understand your strengths and weaknesses

5. What is self-awareness?

   A. Knowing your favorite color
   B. Understanding your emotions, strengths, weaknesses, values, and beliefs
   C. Knowing your favorite food
   D. Understanding your favorite movie

3. SETTING GOALS AND ACTING

The Importance of Goal Setting

Benefits of Setting Goals

Setting goals is a fundamental step in achieving personal mastery and success. Goals provide direction and purpose, acting as a roadmap for where you want to go in life. They help to focus your attention and efforts on what is important, making it easier to allocate your time and resources effectively. By setting goals, you create a vision for your future and establish a plan to make that vision a reality.

Goals also serve as a motivational tool. When you set a goal, you commit to working towards something that is meaningful to you. This commitment can inspire you to push through challenges and persist when faced with obstacles. Additionally, achieving your goals can boost your self-confidence and self-esteem, as each accomplishment reinforces your belief in your abilities.

Another benefit of setting goals is that it enables you to measure progress. Without goals, it can be difficult to gauge how far you've come and how much further you need to go. Goals provide a way to assess your achievements and reflect on your growth over time. This reflection can be incredibly rewarding and can fuel your desire to set and achieve even more ambitious goals in the future.

Goal Setting and Personal Mastery

Personal mastery is about having a deep understanding of yourself and a commitment to personal growth. Goal setting is a critical component of personal mastery because it requires self-awareness to identify what you truly want to achieve. It also demands discipline and perseverance to work towards your goals, even when progress is slow or difficult.

When you practice goal setting, you are actively shaping your future. You are not leaving your development to chance; instead, you are taking control and making deliberate choices about the direction of your life. This proactive approach is at the heart of personal mastery. It empowers you to transform your dreams into actionable steps and, ultimately, into tangible results.

Moreover, goal setting is a skill that improves with practice. As you set and achieve goals, you learn more about what strategies work best for you, how to overcome specific challenges, and how to stay motivated. This learning process is invaluable for personal mastery, as it equips you with the knowledge and skills to tackle future goals with greater confidence and effectiveness.

Understanding Goals

What is a Goal?

A goal is a desired result that a person envisions, plans, and commits to achieve. It is an endpoint of a journey or a specific accomplishment that one strives to attain. Goals can vary greatly in scope and complexity, from simple tasks that can be completed in a short time to long-term aspirations that require years of dedication.

Goals are often specific, measurable, attainable, relevant, and time-bound (SMART). This framework helps to clarify your intentions and provides a clear criterion for tracking your progress. By defining your goals with these characteristics, you increase the likelihood of achieving them.

Types of Goals

Goals can be categorized in several ways, including by duration or by area of life. Short-term goals are those that you can achieve soon, such as completing a project by the end of the week. Long-term goals require more time and planning, such as graduating from high school with honors or getting accepted into a desired college program.

Additionally, goals can be personal, professional, academic, or related to personal interests and hobbies. Personal goals might include improving your health, developing a new skill, or building stronger relationships. Professional or academic goals could involve advancing in your career or excelling in your studies. Goals related to interests and hobbies might be about achieving a certain level of proficiency in a musical instrument or sport.

Characteristics of Effective Goals

Effective goals share certain characteristics that make them more likely to be achieved. They are clear and specific, leaving no ambiguity about what is to be accomplished. They are measurable, meaning there is a way to assess whether the goal has been met. Effective goals are also achievable; they are realistic and attainable with the resources and time available.

Furthermore, effective goals are relevant to your life and aligned with your values and long-term objectives. They are time-bound, with a deadline that creates a sense of urgency and helps prevent procrastination. Lastly, effective goals are flexible enough to adapt to changing circumstances, yet firm enough to serve as a steady guide.

Setting Personal Goals

Identifying Your Personal Goals

Identifying your personal goals begins with self-reflection. Consider what matters most to you, what you want to achieve, and where you see yourself in the future. Think about areas of your life where you feel a strong desire for improvement or change. Reflect on your passions and interests, as these can provide powerful motivation for setting and pursuing goals.

It can be helpful to write down your thoughts and ideas, as this process can clarify your goals and make them more tangible. Don't be afraid to dream big, but also be mindful of what is realistically achievable. Remember that your goals are personal to you and should reflect your unique aspirations and values.

Setting Realistic Goals

While it's important to aim high, setting realistic goals is key to avoiding frustration and disappointment. A realistic goal is one that challenges you but is still attainable with the resources and time you have. To determine if a goal is realistic, consider your current abilities, the obstacles you might face, and the support you have available.

If a goal seems too daunting, break it down into smaller, more manageable steps. These smaller goals can serve as milestones on the way to achieving your larger objective. Celebrating these incremental achievements can provide ongoing motivation and a sense of progress.

Aligning Goals with Values and Interests

Goals that are aligned with your values and interests are more meaningful and engaging. When your goals reflect what you truly care about, you are more likely to commit to them and persevere through challenges. To align your goals with your values, consider what principles are most important to you and how your goals support those principles.

Similarly, incorporating your interests into your goals can make the pursuit more enjoyable and less of a chore. If you're passionate about a particular subject or activity, setting goals related to that interest can be a natural and fulfilling way to grow and develop.

Michael Phelps, the most decorated Olympian of all time, is a prime example of someone who aligned his goals with his values and interests. From a young age, Phelps had a passion for swimming, and he set goals that reflected this interest.

Setting Personal Goals

Phelps set his first goal when he was just 11 years old. He wanted to become a professional swimmer and compete in the Olympics. This goal was not only aligned with his interest in swimming but also with his values of hard work, discipline, and perseverance.

Persevering Through Challenges

Phelps faced many challenges on his journey, including a diagnosis of ADHD and struggles with mental health. However, because his goals were so closely aligned with his values and interests, he was able to persevere and achieve his dreams.

Achieving Success

Phelps' commitment to his goals led him to become the most successful Olympian in history, with a total of 28 medals, 23 of them gold. His story is a powerful example of the potential that can be unlocked when personal goals align with values and interests.

Planning for Goals

Creating a Goal Action Plan –

"A goal without a plan is just a wish" - Antoine de Saint-Exupéry

A goal action plan is a detailed strategy that outlines the steps you need to take to achieve your goal. It includes specific actions, resources required, potential obstacles, and strategies for overcoming those obstacles. An effective action plan also has a timeline that specifies when each step should be completed.

To create your action plan, start by breaking your goal down into smaller tasks. Assign deadlines to these tasks and determine what resources you'll need, such as time, money, information, or assistance from others. Anticipate challenges you might encounter and plan how you will address them. This proactive approach can help you stay on track and adjust as needed.

Setting Timelines for Goals

Timelines are crucial for maintaining momentum and ensuring progress towards your goals. A timeline provides structure and helps you manage your time effectively. When setting timelines, be realistic about how long tasks will take and consider other commitments you have.

For long-term goals, create a series of interim deadlines to keep you moving forward. These interim deadlines can help prevent procrastination and make a large goal feel more achievable. Remember to review and adjust your timelines as necessary, especially if your circumstances change.

Identifying Resources for Goals

Identifying the resources you need is an essential part of planning for your goals. Resources can include books, websites, equipment, financial support, or advice from knowledgeable individuals. Take stock of what you already have and what you'll need to acquire.

Don't overlook the importance of social resources, such as support from family, friends, teachers, or mentors. These individuals can offer encouragement, advice, and practical help. They can also hold you accountable and help you stay committed to your goals.

Acting

Moving from Planning to Action

Once you have a plan in place, it's time to act. Start by tackling the first steps in your action plan. Taking even small actions can build momentum and help you gain confidence. Focus on what you can do today to move closer to your goal, rather than becoming overwhelmed by the entire journey ahead.

As you act, stay flexible and be prepared to adjust your plan. You may encounter unexpected challenges or opportunities that require you to rethink your approach. Being adaptable will help you navigate these changes and keep progressing towards your goal.

"Stay rigid in your vision, but flexible in the execution" – Chris Dessi

Staying Motivated to Achieve Goals

Staying motivated can be challenging, especially when progress is slow or when you face setbacks. To maintain motivation, remind yourself of why your goal is important to you. Visualize the benefits of achieving your goal and the positive impact it will have on your life.

Setting and celebrating small milestones can also help sustain motivation. Each milestone achieved is a step closer to your ultimate goal and a reason to celebrate. Additionally, sharing your goals with others can provide a sense of accountability and encouragement to keep going.

Handling Setbacks in Goal Achievement

Setbacks are a normal part of the goal achievement process. When you encounter a setback, take the time to understand what went wrong and why. Use this information to learn and grow, rather than becoming discouraged.

It's important to maintain a positive attitude and to view setbacks as opportunities for improvement. Adjust your action plan if necessary and recommit to your goal with renewed determination. Remember that perseverance is key to overcoming obstacles and achieving success.

Monitoring Progress

Tracking Goal Progress

Tracking your progress is essential for staying on course and maintaining motivation. Keep a record of the tasks you've completed and the milestones you've reached. This record can be a source of encouragement, showing you how far you've come and what you've accomplished.

There are many ways to track progress, such as using a journal, a spreadsheet, or a goal-tracking app. Choose a method that works best for you and that you'll use consistently. Regularly reviewing your progress can help you stay focused and make necessary adjustments to your plan.

Adjusting Goals as Needed

As you work towards your goals, you may find that some aspects of your plan need to be adjusted. This could be due to changes in your circumstances, new information, or insights gained from experience. Be open to revising your goals and action plan to reflect these changes.

Adjusting your goals is not a sign of failure; it's a sign of flexibility and responsiveness to your evolving needs and environment. By being willing to adapt, you increase your chances of achieving your goals in a way that is meaningful and satisfying.

Celebrating Goal Achievements

Celebrating your achievements is an important part of the goal-setting process. It acknowledges your hard work and dedication, and it reinforces the positive behaviors that led to your success. Celebrations can be as simple as taking a moment to reflect on your accomplishment or as elaborate as throwing a party.

Whatever form your celebration takes, make sure it's meaningful to you. Celebrating your achievements can boost your morale and inspire you to set new goals, continuing your journey of personal growth and mastery.

The Role of Self-Discipline in Goal Achievement

Understanding Self-Discipline

Self-discipline is the ability to control your feelings and overcome weaknesses; it's the ability to pursue what you think is right despite temptations to abandon it. In the context of goal achievement, self-discipline is what enables you to stick to your action plan and work towards your goals, even when it's challenging or when you'd rather be doing something else.

Self-discipline is like a muscle; the more you use it, the stronger it becomes. It involves setting standards for yourself and making commitments that you strive to keep. It's about making choices that align with your goals and values, rather than giving in to short-term gratification or distractions.

Developing Self-Discipline

Developing self-discipline starts with small, manageable changes to your behavior. Begin by setting clear rules for yourself related to your goals. For example, if your goal is to improve your grades, you might set a rule that you will study for a certain number of hours each day.

It's also important to create an environment that supports your self-discipline. This might involve removing temptations or distractions that could lead you off course. Additionally, building a routine can help reinforce self-discipline, as it turns productive behaviors into habits.

Self-Discipline and Goal Achievement

Self-discipline is a key factor in achieving your goals. It helps you stay focused on your action plan and resist the urge to procrastinate or give up. With self-discipline, you can push through moments of doubt or laziness and continue making progress towards your goals.

Moreover, the self-discipline you develop while working towards one goal can benefit other areas of your life. As you strengthen your self-discipline, you'll find it easier to tackle new challenges and pursue additional goals, furthering your journey to personal mastery.

- How does self-discipline help you resist the urge to procrastinate or give up?
- How can the self-discipline you develop while working towards one goal benefit other areas of your life?
- Give an example of a situation where you used self-discipline to overcome a challenge or achieve a goal.

Remember: There are no right or wrong answers. The purpose of these questions is to help you reflect on your understanding of self-discipline and its importance in personal mastery.

Case Studies on Goal Setting and Acting

Real-Life Examples of Goal Setting and Acting

Case studies of individuals who have successfully set and

achieved their goals can provide valuable insights and inspiration. For example, consider the story of a teenager who set a goal to become a better public speaker. By joining a debate club, practicing regularly, and seeking feedback, they were able to overcome their fear of speaking in front of an audience and eventually won a regional debate competition.

Another case study might involve a student who set a goal to improve their physical fitness. They created a workout plan, tracked their progress, and adjusted their goals as they became stronger. Their dedication not only led to improved fitness but also to increased self-confidence and discipline.

Lessons Learned from Case Studies

Case studies often reveal common themes and lessons about goal setting and taking action. One key lesson is the importance of persistence. Many successful individuals faced setbacks and challenges but remained committed to their goals. Their stories demonstrate that perseverance can lead to remarkable achievements.

Another lesson is the value of planning and preparation. Those who took the time to create detailed action plans and anticipate potential obstacles were better equipped to navigate the path to their goals. Additionally, the support of others, whether from friends, family, or mentors, played a significant role in many success stories.

Albert Schweitzer, a renowned philosopher and physician, believed that happiness and success are intertwined. By finding joy in what you do, you increase your chances of achieving success.

Activities for Goal Setting and Acting

Practical Exercises for Goal Setting

Engaging in practical exercises can help you develop the skills needed for effective goal setting. One exercise is to write down your goals using the SMART criteria, ensuring they are specific, measurable, achievable, relevant, and time bound. Another exercise is to create a vision board that visually represents your goals and aspirations, serving as a daily reminder and source of inspiration.

Role-playing scenarios can also be a useful exercise. Imagine yourself facing potential obstacles to your goals and practice how you would respond. This can help you prepare for real-life challenges and build confidence in your ability to overcome them.

Action-Oriented Activities for Goal Achievement

Action-oriented activities are designed to move you from planning to doing. One activity is to establish a daily or weekly routine that incorporates tasks related to your goals. For example, if your goal is to learn a new language, you might set aside time each day for language study and practice.

Another activity is to find an accountability partner who will check in with you regularly about your progress. This can help keep you on track and motivated. You can also join a group or community of people with similar goals, providing a network of support and shared experiences.

The Role of Support in Goal Achievement

Seeking Support for Goals

Seeking support from others can make a significant difference in achieving your goals. Support can come in many forms, such as encouragement, advice, or practical help. Don't hesitate to reach out to family, friends, teachers, or mentors when you need assistance or a morale boost.

---

1. What is one of the benefits of setting goals?

    A. It helps you stay focused and motivated.
    B. It guarantees success in all endeavors.
    C. It allows you to avoid making decisions.
    D. It eliminates the need for self-discipline.

2. What is a characteristic of an effective goal?

    A. It is based on other people's expectations.
    B. It is specific and measurable.
    C. It is vague and general.
    D. It is impossible to achieve.

3. What is the role of self-discipline in goal achievement?

    A. Self-discipline is only important for people with low motivation.
    B. Self-discipline helps you stay on track and resist distractions.
    C. Self-discipline is not necessary if you have a good plan.
    D. Self-discipline only matters for large, long-term goals.

4. What is the role of a mentor in goal achievement?

    A. A mentor should do the work for you.
    B. A mentor is not necessary if you have self-discipline.
    C. A mentor can provide guidance, support, and inspiration.
    D. A mentor should set your goals for you.

5. How does achieving goals build self-confidence?

A. Achieving goals proves that you are better than others.
B. Achieving goals means you no longer need to set goals in the future.
C. Achieving goals eliminates the need for self-improvement.
D. Achieving goals demonstrates your ability to set and meet your own standards.

4. OVERCOMING CHALLENGES

Understanding Challenges

What is a Challenge?

A challenge is a situation or task that requires a person to stretch their abilities and skills to overcome it. It is an obstacle that stands in the way of achieving a goal or making progress. Challenges can be external, such as a difficult exam or a sports competition, or internal, like overcoming shyness or managing time effectively. They demand effort, creativity, and perseverance to be surmounted.

Types of Challenges

Challenges come in various forms and can be categorized in several ways.
Some common types include:

- Physical Challenges: Tasks that require bodily effort, such as running a marathon or climbing a mountain.

- Mental Challenges: Problems that need intellectual effort to solve, like puzzles or complex calculations.

- Emotional Challenges: Situations that test one's ability to manage emotions, such as dealing with loss or rejection.

- Social Challenges: Difficulties in interacting with others, which might include making new friends or resolving conflicts.

The Role of Challenges in Personal Growth

Challenges play a crucial role in personal growth. They push individuals out of their comfort zones, prompting them to develop new skills and gain new insights. Each challenge overcome is a step towards becoming a more resilient and capable person. Moreover, facing and overcoming challenges can lead to increased self-esteem and a sense of accomplishment.

Facing Challenges

Approaching Challenges Positively

Approaching challenges with a positive attitude is essential. A positive approach means seeing challenges as opportunities for growth rather than insurmountable obstacles. It involves maintaining a hopeful outlook and trusting in one's ability to prevail.

Strategies for Facing Challenges

There are several strategies that can help individuals face challenges effectively:

- Breaking Down the Challenge: Dividing a large challenge into smaller, manageable parts can make it less daunting.

- Planning: Developing a clear plan of action with specific steps can provide a roadmap to overcoming the challenge.

- Learning from Others: Seeking advice from those who have faced similar challenges can provide valuable insights and strategies.

- Staying Flexible: Being willing to adapt and change plans as needed is crucial when unexpected issues arise.

Learning from Challenges

Challenges are not just obstacles to overcome; they are also valuable learning experiences. By reflecting on the process of facing a challenge, individuals can gain knowledge about themselves and the world around them. This reflection can lead to improved problem-solving skills and better preparation for future challenges.

Problem-Solving Skills

Understanding Problem-Solving

Problem-solving is the process of identifying a problem, generating possible solutions, and implementing the best solution. It is a critical skill for overcoming challenges of all kinds.

Steps in Problem-Solving

The problem-solving process typically involves the following steps:

1. Identify the Problem: Clearly define the challenge and what needs to be addressed.

2. Analyze the Problem: Gather information and understand the factors involved.

3. Generate Solutions: Brainstorm a list of possible solutions without judging them.

4. Evaluate Solutions: Assess the pros and cons of each solution.

5. Choose a Solution: Select the most feasible and effective solution.

6. Implement the Solution: Put the chosen solution into action.

7. Review the Outcome: Evaluate the results and learn from the experience.

Applying Problem-Solving Skills to Challenges

Applying problem-solving skills to challenges involves being systematic and thoughtful. It requires patience, as the first solution attempted may not always work. It is important to remain persistent and use setbacks as learning opportunities to refine the approach.

Further Reading

Expand your knowledge and improve your problem-solving skills with these recommended books:

1. "The Teen's Guide to World Domination" by Josh Shipp: This book offers valuable advice on how to deal with life's challenges and become the best version of yourself.

2. "The 7 Habits of Highly Effective Teens" by Sean Covey: This book provides a step-by-step guide to help teens improve self-image, build friendships, resist peer pressure, and achieve their goals.

3. "How to Win Friends and Influence People for Teen Girls" by Donna Dale Carnegie: This book offers concrete advice on teen topics such as peer pressure, gossip, and popularity.

Remember: The more you read, the more tools you'll have to overcome any challenge that comes your way!

Resilience in Overcoming Challenges

What is Resilience?

Resilience is the ability to bounce back from setbacks, adapt to change, and keep going in the face of adversity. It is a quality that allows individuals to recover from challenges stronger and more resourceful than before.

Building Resilience

Building resilience is a process that involves:

- Developing a Support Network: Having a group of friends, family, or mentors to turn to for encouragement and advice.

- Maintaining a Positive Outlook: Focusing on the positives and remaining hopeful even when faced with difficulties.

- Learning from Experience: Reflecting on past challenges and the strategies that helped overcome them.

- Practicing Self-Care: Taking care of one's physical and emotional wellbeing to stay strong during tough times.

Resilience and Overcoming Challenges

Resilience is key to overcoming challenges. It enables individuals to confront difficulties with confidence and to persevere until they reach their goals. Resilient people view challenges as temporary and believe in their capacity to overcome them.

Coping Strategies

Understanding Coping Strategies

Coping strategies are the methods people use to deal with stress and adversity. They can be healthy, such as exercising or talking to a friend, or unhealthy, like avoidance or substance abuse. Effective coping strategies help individuals manage their emotions and maintain their well-being in the face of challenges.

Effective Coping Strategies for Challenges

Some effective coping strategies include:

- Stress Reduction Techniques: Activities like meditation, deep breathing, or yoga that help reduce stress.

- Positive Reappraisal: Reframing a challenge in a positive light to find the hidden opportunities.

- Seeking Help: Asking for assistance when a challenge seems too difficult to handle alone.

- Time Management: Organizing time effectively to manage tasks and reduce overwhelm.

Adapting Coping Strategies to Different Challenges

Not all coping strategies work for every challenge. It is important to assess the situation and choose strategies that are most appropriate for the specific challenge at hand. Flexibility and willingness to try new approaches are key to finding effective coping mechanisms.

The Role of Support in Overcoming Challenges

Seeking Support When Facing Challenges

Seeking support from others can provide encouragement, advice, and a different perspective on a challenge. Support can come from friends, family, teachers, counselors, or support groups. It is a sign of strength to recognize when help is needed and to reach out for it.

The Role of Mentors and Role Models in Overcoming Challenges

Mentors and role models can play a significant role in overcoming challenges. They can offer guidance, share their own experiences, and serve as an example of how to navigate difficulties successfully. Having a mentor or role model can also provide motivation and inspiration to persevere.

Case Studies on Overcoming Challenges

Real-Life Examples of Overcoming Challenges

Real-life examples of individuals or groups who have overcome significant challenges can be powerful learning tools. These stories illustrate the strategies and mindsets that can lead to success in the face of adversity.

Lessons Learned from Case Studies

Case studies often reveal common themes, such as the importance of resilience, the value of a support network, and the effectiveness of a positive attitude. They can also highlight the diverse ways in which people approach and overcome challenges, providing a range of strategies to draw from.

Activities for Overcoming Challenges

Practical Exercises for Overcoming Challenges

Practical exercises, such as role-playing difficult situations or practicing problem-solving skills, can help individuals prepare for and overcome challenges. These activities allow for hands-on experience in a safe environment.

Reflective Activities on Challenges

Reflective activities, like journaling or group discussions, can help individuals process their experiences with challenges and learn from them. Reflection is a key component of turning challenges into opportunities for growth.

Quick Facts & Statistics

Challenges and Teenagers

Did you know?

> According to the American Psychological Association, nearly half of all teenagers (45%) believe they are under a lot of stress.
>
> A study by the National Institute of Mental Health found that 1 in 3 teenagers will experience an anxiety disorder.
>
> Research shows that journaling can reduce stress and improve mental health. A study published in the Journal of Adolescence found that teenagers who journal regularly showed reduced symptoms of stress and depression.

Group discussions are also beneficial. According to a study by the University of Illinois, teenagers who participate in group discussions about challenges and stressors report feeling less alone and more understood.

Turning Challenges into Opportunities

Interesting Facts:

1. Research from the University of Pennsylvania found that teenagers who view challenges as opportunities for growth are more likely to succeed academically.

2. A study by Stanford University found that teenagers who embrace challenges are more likely to have a 'growth mindset', which is linked to greater life satisfaction and achievement.

Overcoming Challenges and Self-Confidence

How Overcoming Challenges Builds Self-Confidence

Each challenge overcome serves as evidence of one's abilities, which in turn builds self-confidence. Success breeds confidence, and as individuals face and conquer more challenges, their belief in their own capabilities grows.

The Interplay Between Self-Confidence and Overcoming Challenges

Self-confidence and overcoming challenges have a reciprocal relationship. Confidence can make it easier to face challenges, while successfully navigating challenges can enhance self-confidence. This positive cycle can lead to a more empowered and self-assured individual.

The Power of Overcoming Challenges

Reflecting on the Journey of Overcoming Challenges

Reflecting on the journey of overcoming challenges can provide valuable insights into personal strengths and areas for growth. It can also reinforce the lessons learned and the strategies that were effective, preparing individuals for future challenges.

Looking Forward: Overcoming Challenges in the Journey to Mastery

Overcoming challenges is an integral part of the journey to personal mastery. Each challenge faced and conquered contributes to the development of a stronger, more capable, and more resilient individual. Looking forward, the skills and confidence gained from overcoming challenges will be invaluable assets in the continuous pursuit of personal growth and mastery.

This is why sports can be so important in a teenagers development. You're exposed to the reality that there will always be challenges. You'll strike out, give up a goal, cause a penalty, miss the shot etc. This ability to experience something percieved as a negative, let it wash over you, and continue to march on is critical on your journey to self mastery.

Just keep moving forward.

1. What is the role of challenges in personal growth?

    A. Challenges are irrelevant to personal growth.
    B. Challenges have no impact on personal growth.
    C. Challenges hinder personal growth.
    D. Challenges provide opportunities for learning and growth.

2. What is a key step in problem-solving?

    A. Ignoring the problem
    B. Understanding the problem
    C. Blaming others for the problem

    D. Avoiding the problem

3. What is resilience?

    A. The ability to create challenges
    B. The ability to ignore challenges
    C. The ability to bounce back from challenges

    D. The ability to avoid challenges

4. What is the role of mentors and role models in overcoming challenges?

    A. They create more challenges.
    B. They provide guidance and support.
    C. They discourage you from facing challenges.

    D. They have no role in overcoming challenges.

5. How does overcoming challenges build self-confidence?

    A. Overcoming challenges only builds self-confidence if someone else acknowledges your success.

B. Overcoming challenges reduces self-confidence because it is difficult.
C. Overcoming challenges proves to yourself that you are capable, which builds self-confidence.
D. It doesn't. Overcoming challenges and self-confidence are unrelated.

5. BUILDING CONFIDENCE AND SELF-ESTEEM

Understanding Confidence and Self-Esteem

What is Confidence?

Confidence is the belief in one's own abilities and judgment. It is the feeling of certainty that you can accomplish what you set out to do. Confidence is not about being the best, but rather about being secure in your skills and talents. It's the internal sense of self-assurance that allows you to take risks, face challenges, and interact with others assertively. Confidence can vary from situation to situation; you may feel confident in your ability to solve math problems, but less so in social settings.

Confidence is dynamic, changing with experience and success. Each time you try something new and succeed, your confidence grows. Conversely, setbacks can temporarily shake your confidence. However, with the right mindset, you can learn from failure and rebuild your confidence even stronger than before.

What is Self-Esteem?

Self-esteem is your overall opinion of yourself — how you feel about your abilities and limitations. When you have healthy self-esteem, you feel good about yourself and see yourself as deserving the respect of others. When you have low self-esteem, you put little value on your opinions and ideas and may find yourself constantly battling self-doubt.

Unlike confidence, which can fluctuate, self-esteem tends to be a more consistent and long-term feeling. It's shaped by your thoughts, relationships, and experiences throughout your life. Building self-esteem is about developing a positive and realistic perception of who you are.

Self-esteem is earned. Through grit, tenasity and persistence.

The Relationship Between Confidence and Self-Esteem

Confidence and self-esteem are closely related, but they are not the same thing. Confidence is specific to particular tasks or abilities, while selfesteem is a general sense of self-worth. You can be confident in your ability to do well on a test because you've studied hard, but still have low self-esteem if you believe that your worth as a person hinges on the outcome of that test.

High self-esteem can contribute to confidence, as feeling good about who you are can make you more willing to try new things. Conversely, acting confidently and experiencing success can boost your self-esteem. Together, they form a virtuous cycle that can lead to personal growth and fulfillment.

Further Reading

Want to dive deeper into the world of confidence and self-esteem? Here are some excellent books that can help you understand these concepts better and guide you on your journey to personal mastery:

1. "The Six Pillars of Self-Esteem" by Nathaniel Branden: This book provides a comprehensive look at what self-esteem is and how to improve it.

2. "The Confidence Code: The Science and Art of Self-Assurance What Women Should Know" by Katty Kay and Claire Shipman: A great read for young girls, this book explores the concept of confidence and provides practical advice on how to build it.

3. "Daring Greatly: How the Courage to Be Vulnerable Transforms the Way We Live, Love, Parent, and Lead" by Brené Brown: This book explores the relationship between vulnerability and selfesteem, and how embracing our imperfections can lead to increased confidence.

4. "Mindset: The New Psychology of Success" by Carol S. Dweck: This book introduces the concept of "growth mindset," which can help boost both confidence and self-esteem.

Remember, the journey to personal mastery is a lifelong one. Keep learning, keep growing, and most importantly, believe in yourself!

The Importance of Confidence and Self-Esteem

Benefits of High Confidence and Self-Esteem

High confidence and self-esteem have numerous benefits. They allow you to face life with a positive attitude and the resilience to bounce back from setbacks. With high confidence, you're more likely to take on new challenges and persevere until you succeed. High self-esteem gives you the strength to stand up for yourself and make decisions that are right for you, without undue influence from others.

Together, confidence and self-esteem can improve your mental health, leading to lower levels of stress and anxiety. They can also enhance your relationships, as you're more likely to communicate effectively and assertively. In school, high confidence and self-esteem can lead to better performance, as you're more willing to participate in class and take on challenging projects.

Confidence, Self-Esteem and Personal Mastery

Personal mastery is about living life to the fullest and realizing your potential. Confidence and self-esteem are foundational to this pursuit. With confidence, you can develop your talents and skills to their highest levels. With self-esteem, you can appreciate your unique qualities and contributions to the world.

Personal mastery involves setting and achieving goals, which requires both confidence and self-esteem. Confidence gives you the courage to set ambitious goals, while self-esteem helps you value your achievements and learn from your failures. Together, they empower you to take control of your life and steer it in the direction you choose.

Building Confidence

Strategies for Building Confidence

Building confidence starts with setting achievable goals and working towards them. Start small and gradually take on bigger challenges as your confidence grows. It's also important to prepare thoroughly for tasks, as being well-prepared can make you feel more confident.

Another key strategy is to focus on your successes, no matter how small. Celebrate your achievements and learn from your mistakes without letting them define you. Surround yourself with supportive people who believe in you and avoid those who undermine your confidence.

Practicing Confidence-Building Activities

There are many activities you can do to build confidence. Public speaking, for example, is a powerful way to boost confidence. Joining a club or team can also help, as it provides opportunities to develop skills and achieve goals in a supportive environment.

Practicing assertiveness is another effective activity. This means expressing your thoughts and feelings in a respectful but firm manner. It can be as simple as voicing your opinion in a group discussion or standing up for yourself when necessary.

Maintaining Confidence Over Time

Maintaining confidence over time requires a commitment to continuous learning and growth. Keep challenging yourself with new goals and seek out experiences that push you out of your comfort zone.

It's also important to maintain a positive attitude, even in the face of setbacks. Learn to view failures as opportunities to learn and grow, rather than as reflections of your worth. Regularly reflect on your achievements and the progress you've made and remind yourself of your strengths and abilities.

Building Self-Esteem

Strategies for Building Self-Esteem

Building self-esteem involves changing how you perceive and value yourself. Start by challenging negative beliefs about yourself and replacing them with positive affirmations. Focus on your strengths and accomplishments and forgive yourself for past mistakes.

It's also helpful to set boundaries and learn to say no. This shows that you value your own needs and time. Engaging in activities that make you feel good about yourself, such as volunteering or learning a new skill, can also boost self-esteem.

Practicing Self-Esteem-Building Activities

There are many activities that can help build self-esteem. Keeping a journal where you write down things you like about yourself, and your accomplishments can reinforce positive self-perceptions. Engaging in physical exercise can also improve self-esteem, as it not only makes you feel better physically but also gives you a sense of achievement.

Practicing self-care is another important activity. This means taking time for yourself, whether it's reading a book, taking a bath, or meditating. Selfcare shows that you value and respect yourself.

Maintaining Self-Esteem Over Time

Maintaining self-esteem over time requires regular self-reflection and self-compassion. Acknowledge your worth regularly and be kind to yourself, especially when you're facing challenges. Surround yourself with positive influences and people who appreciate you for who you are.

It's also important to continue setting and achieving goals, as this gives you a sense of purpose and accomplishment. Remember to be patient with yourself; building and maintaining self-esteem is a lifelong process. Your goals can be as small as remembering to make your bed. Or as big as get accepted into your dream University.

Sometimes the voice in our head can be the most critical. Remember to be gentle with yourself as you work through this book. You're trying your best.

Overcoming Confidence and Self-Esteem Challenges

Identifying Confidence and Self-Esteem Challenges

The first step in overcoming confidence and self-esteem challenges is to identify them. This might involve recognizing patterns of negative self-talk, understanding the situations that make you feel less confident, or acknowledging past experiences that have impacted your self-esteem.

Once you've identified these challenges, you can begin to address them. This might involve seeking feedback from trusted friends or mentors, reflecting on your thoughts and behaviors, and being mindful of your reactions to different situations.

Strategies for Overcoming Confidence and Self-Esteem Challenges

There are several strategies to overcome confidence and self-esteem challenges. One effective approach is cognitive restructuring, which involves identifying and challenging negative thoughts and replacing them with more positive and realistic ones.

Another strategy is to engage in activities that build mastery and competence. By developing new skills and achieving success in different areas, you can improve your self-image and feel more capable.

Seeking Support for Confidence and Self-Esteem Challenges

Seeking support from others can be incredibly helpful when working on confidence and self-esteem challenges. This might involve talking to a counselor or therapist, joining a support group, or simply having open conversations with friends or family members.

Support from others can provide encouragement, offer new perspectives, and help you feel less alone in your struggles. It can also provide accountability as you work on building your confidence and self-esteem.

The Role of Positive Self-Talk

Understanding Positive Self-Talk

Positive self-talk is the practice of speaking to yourself in an encouraging and supportive way. It involves focusing on your strengths and accomplishments, rather than dwelling on mistakes or perceived flaws.

Positive self-talk can help shift your mindset from one of criticism and doubt to one of optimism and self-belief. It's a powerful tool for building confidence and self-esteem because it directly influences how you perceive yourself.

Practicing Positive Self-Talk

Practicing positive self-talk involves being aware of your internal dialogue and consciously choosing words that are kind and affirming. Start by noticing when you engage in negative self-talk and gently correct yourself with positive statements.

You can also create affirmations that resonate with you and repeat them regularly. These affirmations should be in the present tense, positive, and specific to your goals and values.

Positive Self-Talk and Confidence and Self-Esteem

Positive self-talk can significantly impact your confidence and self-esteem.
By affirming your abilities and worth, you reinforce your belief in yourself. This can lead to a more positive self-image and greater confidence in your abilities to face challenges and achieve your goals.

Over time, positive self-talk can become a habit, leading to lasting improvements in how you view yourself and your capabilities.

Case Studies on Building Confidence and Self-Esteem

Real-Life Examples of Building Confidence and

Self-Esteem

There are many inspiring real-life examples of individuals who have successfully built their confidence and self-esteem. These stories often involve overcoming significant obstacles, such as bullying, failure, or self-doubt, and demonstrate the transformative power of self-belief and perseverance.

By studying these case studies, you can learn about the strategies and mindsets that have helped others succeed and apply these lessons to your own life.

Lessons Learned from Case Studies

One common lesson from these case studies is the importance of persistence. Building confidence and self-esteem is a process that takes time and effort, and setbacks are a normal part of the journey.

Another lesson is the value of support from others. Whether it's a mentor, friend, or family member, having someone who believes in you can make a significant difference in your ability to overcome challenges and build self-esteem.

"I can't change the direction of the wind, but I can adjust my sails to always reach my destination." - Jimmy Dean

This quote reminds us that while we can't control everything that happens to us, we can control how we respond. This is a key aspect of building confidence and self-esteem.

"It's not what you are that holds you back, it's what you think you are not." - Denis Waitley

Waitley's quote underscores the importance of positive selfperception. If you believe you lack certain qualities, it can hinder your progress. But if you focus on your strengths, you can build your confidence and self-esteem.

"The only person you are destined to become is the person you decide to be." - Ralph Waldo Emerson

Emerson's quote highlights the power of personal choice. You have the power to shape your own destiny by the choices you make, including the choice to build your confidence and self-esteem.

Activities for Building Confidence and Self-esteem

Practical Exercises for Building Confidence and Self-Esteem

There are many practical exercises you can do to build confidence and self-esteem. For example, setting and achieving small goals can give you a sense of accomplishment and boost your confidence. You can also try roleplaying exercises to practice assertiveness and communication skills.

Visualization is another powerful tool. Imagine yourself succeeding in a challenging situation and focus on the feelings of confidence and pride that come with that success.

Reflective Activities for Building Confidence and Self-Esteem

Reflective activities, such as journaling or meditation, can also help build confidence and self-esteem. These activities allow you to explore your thoughts and feelings, recognize your achievements, and set intentions for personal growth.

Reflecting on your values and how they align with your actions can also reinforce your sense of self-worth and purpose.

Confidence, Self-Esteem and Relationships

How Confidence and Self-Esteem Impact Relationships

Confidence and self-esteem play a crucial role in the health of your relationships. When you feel good about yourself, you're more likely to engage in positive interactions and establish boundaries that protect your well-being.

High self-esteem allows you to be authentic in your relationships, as you're not constantly seeking approval from others. Confidence helps you communicate effectively and assertively, ensuring that your needs are heard and respected.

Building Confidence and Self-Esteem in Relationships

Building confidence and self-esteem in relationships involves being open and honest about your feelings, as well as being willing to listen to and respect the feelings of others. It also means being assertive about your needs and seeking out relationships that are supportive and affirming.

Participating in shared activities and working on common goals can also strengthen your relationships and boost your confidence and self-esteem.

Confidence, Self-Esteem and Goal Achievement

The Role of Confidence and Self-Esteem in Achieving Goals

Confidence and self-esteem are essential for setting and achieving goals. Confidence gives you the belief in your ability to reach your goals, while self-esteem provides the motivation to pursue them because you value yourself and your aspirations.

Together, they enable you to set challenging yet achievable goals, develop plans to reach them, and persevere in the face of obstacles.

Building Confidence and Self-Esteem for Goal Achievement

To build confidence and self-esteem for goal achievement, start by setting clear, specific, and realistic goals. Break these goals down into manageable steps and celebrate your progress along the way.

Surround yourself with positive influences and seek out role models who have achieved similar goals. Their success can inspire you and provide a roadmap for your own journey.

The Power of Confidence and Self-Esteem

Reflecting on the Journey of Building Confidence and
Self-Esteem

Building confidence and self-esteem is a journey that involves self-discovery, growth, and resilience. Reflecting on this journey can help you appreciate how far you've come and the challenges you've overcome.

It's important to recognize that confidence and self-esteem are not static; they can fluctuate and require ongoing attention and nurturing.

Looking Forward: Confidence and Self-Esteem in the
Journey to Mastery

As you continue your journey to personal mastery, remember that confidence and self-esteem are your allies. They will empower you to take on new challenges, develop your talents, and live a fulfilling life.

Keep practicing the strategies and activities outlined in this chapter and be patient with yourself as you grow. With time and effort, you can build the confidence and self-esteem that will support you in all your endeavors.

1. What is the relationship between confidence and self-esteem?

    A. Confidence is a result of high self-esteem
    B. Confidence and self-esteem are the same thing
    C. Confidence and self-esteem are unrelated

D. Self-esteem is a result of high confidence

2. Which of the following is NOT a strategy for building confidence?

   A. Setting and achieving goals
   B. Avoiding challenges
   C. Practicing positive self-talk
   D. Learning new skills

3. How does positive self-talk impact confidence and self-esteem?

   A. It has no impact
   B. It only impacts self-esteem
   C. It can help build and maintain both

   D. It can decrease both

4. What role does confidence play in achieving goals?

   A. Confidence can prevent goal achievement
   B. Confidence can make it easier to take action towards goals
   C. Confidence is not necessary for achieving goals
   D. Confidence ensures goal achievement

5. What is one way to overcome challenges to confidence and self-esteem?

   A. Lower your expectations
   B. Avoid situations that challenge confidence and self-esteem
   C. Seek support from trusted individuals
   D. Ignore the challenges

6. DEVELOPING POSITIVE HABITS

Understanding Habits

What is a Habit?

A habit is a routine behavior that is repeated regularly and tends to occur subconsciously. Habits are automatic responses to specific situations, which can be developed through repetition and practice. Over time, these actions become ingrained in our daily lives, often without us needing to exert conscious thought or effort. Habits can be as simple as brushing your teeth every morning or as complex as the way you communicate with others.

Types of Habits

Habits can be categorized into various types, including good habits, which have a positive impact on our lives, and bad habits, which can be detrimental to our well-being. There are also keystone habits, which can trigger a chain reaction of other good habits due to their foundational nature. For example, regular exercise can lead to better eating habits and improved sleep patterns.

The Role of Habits in Personal Mastery

Habits play a crucial role in the pursuit of personal mastery. They form the foundation of our daily routines and can significantly influence our productivity, health, and overall happiness. By cultivating positive habits, individuals can create a structured and efficient lifestyle, which is essential for achieving personal goals and self-improvement.

Want to delve deeper into the world of habits and personal mastery? Here are some recommended books that can help you understand and develop positive habits:

1. "The Power of Habit" by Charles Duhigg: This book explores the science behind habit creation and reformation. Duhigg explains how habits work and how they can be changed to improve our lives.

2. "Atomic Habits" by James Clear: Clear provides practical strategies for forming good habits, breaking bad ones, and mastering the tiny behaviors that lead to remarkable results.

3. "The 7 Habits of Highly Effective Teens" by Sean Covey: A teen adaptation of Stephen R. Covey's famous "7 Habits of Highly Effective People". This book provides a step-by-step guide to help teens improve self-image, build friendships, resist peer pressure, and achieve their goals.

Remember, knowledge is power. The more you learn about habits and how they shape your life, the better equipped you'll be to make positive changes!

The Importance of Positive Habits

Benefits of Positive Habits

Positive habits are beneficial for several reasons. They can improve our physical health, enhance our mental well-being, and boost our emotional stability. For instance, a habit of regular exercise not only strengthens the body but also releases endorphins that help to reduce stress and increase happiness. Positive habits also contribute to better time management and can lead to a more balanced and fulfilling life.

Positive Habits and Personal Growth

Personal growth is deeply connected to the habits we cultivate. Positive habits encourage a proactive approach to life, fostering a mindset geared towards continuous improvement and learning. They help us to build discipline, focus, and the resilience needed to overcome obstacles. As we replace negative habits with positive ones, we open the door to new opportunities and experiences that contribute to our personal development. Be patient with yourself and celebrate small victories along the way.

Creating Positive Habits

Identifying Positive Habits to Develop

To develop positive habits, it is essential to first identify the areas in your life where you want to see improvement. Reflect on your daily activities and consider which habits could lead to better health, increased productivity, or enhanced relationships. It's important to start with small, manageable habits that align with your overall goals and values.

Steps to Creating a Positive Habit

Creating a positive habit involves several key steps. First, define the habit clearly and understand the benefits it will bring. Next, start small and gradually build up the complexity of the habit. Consistency is crucial, so set specific times and cues to perform the habit. Finally, reinforce the habit with rewards and positive reinforcement to make it stick.

Maintaining Positive Habits Over Time

Maintaining positive habits over time requires persistence and adaptability. Life circumstances can change, and flexibility is needed to sustain habits. It's important to review and adjust your habits regularly to ensure they remain relevant and beneficial. Additionally, having a support system can provide motivation and accountability to help maintain these positive changes.

Overcoming Negative Habits

Identifying Negative Habits to Overcome

Overcoming negative habits begins with recognition. Identify the habits that are hindering your progress or causing harm to your well-being. Understanding the triggers and underlying reasons for these habits is the first step towards change. Be honest with yourself about the impact these habits have on your life and the benefits of eliminating them.

Strategies for Overcoming Negative Habits

To overcome negative habits, it's helpful to replace them with positive alternatives. This can redirect the energy and time spent on the negative habit towards something beneficial. It's also important to change your environment to remove triggers and cues associated with the bad habit. Seeking support from friends, family, or professionals can provide additional motivation and guidance.

Maintaining Progress in Overcoming Negative Habits

Maintaining progress in overcoming negative habits involves regular self-reflection and monitoring. Celebrate small victories to keep yourself motivated, and don't be too hard on yourself if you experience setbacks. Learning from these moments can strengthen your resolve and provide valuable insights into how to avoid future relapses.

The Role of Willpower and Self-Discipline

Understanding Willpower and Self-Discipline

Willpower is the ability to resist short-term temptations in order to meet long-term goals, while self-discipline refers to the practice of training oneself to do things at the right time and in the right way. Both are essential for habit development, as they provide the mental strength needed to stick to positive habits and avoid negative ones.

Building Willpower and Self-Discipline

Building willpower and self-discipline can be achieved through practice and self-awareness. Start with small tasks that require discipline and gradually increase the challenge. Establish routines that reinforce self-control and use techniques such as mindfulness to stay focused on your goals. Remember, willpower is like a muscle; it gets stronger the more you use it.

Willpower, Self-Discipline and Habit Development

Willpower and self-discipline are the foundations of successful habit development. They help you to maintain consistency, even when faced with difficulties or distractions. By cultivating these qualities, you can ensure that your positive habits become a natural and effortless part of your daily life.

Case Studies on Developing Positive Habits

Real-Life Examples of Developing Positive Habits

There are many inspiring real-life examples of individuals who have successfully developed positive habits. These stories often involve overcoming significant challenges and demonstrate the transformative power of consistent, positive actions. By studying these case studies, we can learn valuable lessons about the habit formation process.

Lessons Learned from Case Studies

Case studies on habit development often reveal common themes, such as the importance of setting clear goals, the need for accountability, and the benefits of starting small. They also highlight the role of perseverance and the impact of a supportive environment. By applying these lessons to our own lives, we can enhance our ability to develop and maintain positive habits.

Activities for Developing Positive Habits

Practical Exercises for Developing Positive Habits

Practical exercises can be a fun and effective way to develop positive habits. These activities might include habit tracking, journaling, or participating in challenges that encourage consistent behavior. Engaging in these exercises can help solidify the habit formation process and make it more enjoyable.

Reflective Activities for Habit Development

Reflective activities, such as meditation or guided visualization, can also support habit development. These practices encourage mindfulness and self-awareness, which are crucial for recognizing progress and making necessary adjustments to your habits. Reflection can deepen your understanding of the habits you're trying to build and their significance in your life.

Positive Habits and Self-Confidence

How Developing Positive Habits Builds Self-Confidence

Developing positive habits can significantly boost self-confidence. As you successfully incorporate new habits into your life and witness the positive changes they bring, your belief in your abilities grows. This increased self-confidence can then fuel further positive changes and habit development.

The Interplay Between Self-Confidence and Habit Development

Self-confidence and habit development have a reciprocal relationship. While developing positive habits can enhance self-confidence, having confidence in oneself can also make it easier to establish and stick to new habits. This positive feedback loop can lead to a cycle of continuous improvement and personal growth.

Positive Habits and Relationships

How Positive Habits Impact Relationships

Positive habits can have a profound impact on relationships. Habits such as active listening, expressing gratitude, and showing empathy can strengthen connections with others. Additionally, when you have good habits in place, you're more likely to be reliable and trustworthy, which are key qualities in any healthy relationship.

Developing Positive Habits for Healthy Relationships

Developing habits that promote healthy relationships involves intentional actions and consistent practice. Focus on habits that foster open communication, mutual respect, and shared experiences. By doing so, you can create a strong foundation for lasting and meaningful relationships.

Consistency is Key: It takes an average of 66 days to form a new habit. So, don't be discouraged if you don't see immediate changes. Keep practicing!

Positive Habits Boost Happiness: Studies show that people who practice positive habits, like expressing gratitude or regular exercise, report higher levels of happiness.

Healthy Relationships: Positive habits such as open communication and mutual respect can significantly improve the quality of your relationships.

Success in Life: Successful people often attribute their achievements to the practice of positive habits. These habits include goal setting, planning, and persistence.

Remember, developing positive habits is a journey, not a destination.
Keep exploring, learning, and growing!

Positive Habits and Goal Achievement

The Role of Positive Habits in Achieving Goals

Positive habits are instrumental in achieving goals. They provide the structure and routine needed to make consistent progress, and they help to automate behaviors that lead to success. By aligning your habits with your goals, you can ensure that every action you take moves you closer to your desired outcome.

Developing Positive Habits for Goal Achievement

To develop habits that support goal achievement, start by breaking down your goals into specific, actionable steps. Then, create habits around these steps, ensuring that they are measurable and time bound. As these habits become ingrained, they will naturally guide you towards accomplishing your goals.

Conclusion: The Power of Positive Habits

Reflecting on the Journey of Developing Positive Habits

The journey of developing positive habits is a rewarding one, filled with personal insights and growth. Reflecting on this journey allows you to appreciate the progress you've made and to understand the value of the habits you've cultivated. It's a process that requires commitment and patience, but the benefits are well worth the effort.

Looking Forward: Positive Habits in the Journey to Mastery

As you continue on your journey to personal mastery, remember that positive habits are the building blocks of success. They shape your character, influence your actions, and ultimately determine the quality of your life. By focusing on developing and maintaining positive habits, you set the stage for a fulfilling and accomplished future.

1. What is a habit?

    A. A type of food
    B. A repeated action or behavior

    C. A type of exercise

    D. A type of clothing

2. Why are positive habits important?

    A. They help you win games
    B. They make you popular
    C. They help in personal growth

    D. They make you taller

3. What is the role of willpower and self-discipline in developing habits?

    A. They make habits unnecessary

    B. They are not important
    C. They make habits harder to develop

    D. They help in maintaining and developing habits

4. How do positive habits impact relationships?

    A. They can contribute to healthier relationships
    B. They have no impact on relationships
    C. They make relationships more difficult
    D. They make relationships unnecessary

5. What is the role of positive habits in achieving goals?

    A.   They make goals unnecessary
    B.   They can help in achieving goals
    C.   They have no role in achieving goals
    D.   They make goals harder to achieve

7. MANAGING EMOTIONS AND STRESS

Understanding Emotions

What are Emotions?

Emotions are complex psychological states that involve three distinct components: a subjective experience, a physiological response, and a behavioral or expressive response. Emotions are the body's way of signaling what is happening around us and help us react to situations both positively and negatively. They are integral to our daily lives and influence our decisions, actions, and interactions with others.

Emotions can be fleeting, like the irritation you feel when someone interrupts you, or they can be long-lasting, such as the grief experienced after losing a loved one. Understanding emotions is the first step in learning how to manage them effectively, which is a crucial skill for personal mastery and well-being.

Types of Emotions

Psychologists have categorized emotions in various ways. One common method is to divide them into basic and complex emotions. Basic emotions, such as happiness, sadness, fear, disgust, surprise, and anger, are universal and often have a clear and identifiable cause. They are also associated with distinct facial expressions and body language.

Complex emotions, such as jealousy, guilt, pride, and embarrassment, are more nuanced and may be influenced by cultural factors and personal experiences. They often arise from a combination of basic emotions and require a higher level of self-awareness and reflection to understand and manage.

The Role of Emotions in Personal Mastery

Emotions play a vital role in personal mastery, which is the ongoing process of understanding and developing oneself to achieve one's fullest potential. They can serve as a guide, helping us to align our actions with our values and goals. For instance, feeling joy when helping others can reinforce our commitment to altruism.

However, when emotions are intense or unmanaged, they can cloud judgment and lead to impulsive decisions. Learning to recognize, understand, and manage emotions is therefore essential for personal growth and achieving personal mastery.

Understanding Stress

What is Stress?

Stress is the body's response to any demand or challenge. When faced with a stressor, the body reacts with a "fight-or-flight" response, which prepares the body to either confront or flee from the challenge. This response can be beneficial in short bursts, helping us to deal with immediate threats or challenges. However, chronic stress can have detrimental effects on our health and well-being.

Stress can be triggered by a variety of factors, including work pressures, relationship issues, financial difficulties, or health concerns. It's important to recognize that stress is not always negative; it can also come from positive changes in life, such as starting a new job or moving to a new city.

Types of Stress

Stress can be categorized into two main types: acute stress and chronic stress. Acute stress is short-term and is the body's immediate reaction to a new challenge or threat. It's often resolved quickly, and the body returns to a state of homeostasis.

Chronic stress, on the other hand, occurs when stressors persist over an extended period. This type of stress can lead to a range of health issues, including anxiety, depression, cardiovascular diseases, and a weakened immune system. Recognizing the type of stress you're experiencing is crucial for managing it effectively.

The Role of Stress in Personal Mastery

While stress is often viewed negatively, it can also be a powerful motivator and catalyst for growth. It can push individuals to adapt, learn new skills, and overcome obstacles. The key to harnessing stress for personal mastery lies in managing it effectively and maintaining a balance that does not overwhelm one's capacity to cope.

Developing resilience, the ability to bounce back from stress, is an important aspect of personal mastery. It allows individuals to face challenges with confidence and learn from their experiences, leading to personal growth and improved well-being.

Did You Know?

Stress isn't always a bad thing. In fact, it's a normal part of life that can help us develop and grow. Here are some interesting facts about stress:

Positive Stress: Not all stress is harmful. 'Eustress', or positive stress, can motivate us, help us focus our energy, feel excited, and work towards our personal mastery.

Stress and Growth: Stress can lead to personal growth. It can push us out of our comfort zones, forcing us to adapt and learn new skills.

Resilience: The ability to recover from stress, known as resilience, can be developed and strengthened over time. It's like a muscle the more you use it, the stronger it gets!

Stress and Health: While chronic or long-term stress can have negative effects on our health, short-term or acute stress can boost our immune system.

Remember, the key to using stress to your advantage is managing it effectively. So next time you're feeling stressed, think about how it can help you grow and achieve personal mastery!

Emotion Management

Identifying Emotions

The first step in managing emotions is to identify them accurately. This involves paying attention to the physical sensations in your body, the thoughts that are running through your mind, and the way you are behaving in response to those feelings. Keeping an emotion journal can be a helpful tool for recognizing patterns in emotional responses and triggers.

It's also important to differentiate between the emotion itself and the actions it prompts. For example, anger is a natural emotion, but how you choose to express that anger can have very different outcomes. Learning to identify emotions correctly allows for more effective management and expression.

Strategies for Managing Emotions

Once you've identified your emotions, you can employ various strategies to manage them. These strategies might include deep breathing exercises, mindfulness meditation, or cognitive-behavioral techniques such as reframing negative thoughts. It's also beneficial to engage in activities that you enjoy and that bring you a sense of calm, such as reading, drawing, or spending time in nature.

Another key strategy is to communicate your emotions effectively. This involves expressing your feelings in a way that is clear and assertive, without being aggressive. It's about finding a balance between suppressing emotions and letting them out in an uncontrolled way.

Maintaining Emotional Balance Over Time

Maintaining emotional balance is an ongoing process. It requires regular self-reflection and the willingness to adapt your emotion management strategies as your circumstances change. Building a strong support network of friends, family, or counselors can provide additional perspectives and guidance.

Developing a routine that includes time for relaxation and self-care can also help maintain emotional balance. Regular physical activity, adequate sleep, and a balanced diet contribute to overall emotional well-being.

Stress Management

Identifying Stressors

To manage stress effectively, it's important to first identify the sources of stress in your life. These can be external, such as deadlines and social pressures, or internal, such as self-criticism and unrealistic expectations. Keeping a stress diary can help you track when and why you feel stressed and identify patterns or recurring stressors.

Once you've identified your stressors, you can begin to develop strategies to address them. This might involve problem-solving techniques, time management skills, or seeking support from others.

Strategies for Managing Stress

There are many strategies for managing stress, and what works for one person may not work for another. Some effective stress management techniques include exercise, which can help reduce the physical tension associated with stress, and relaxation techniques like yoga or meditation, which can help calm the mind.

Time management is also crucial for reducing stress. Prioritizing tasks, breaking down large projects into smaller steps, and setting realistic deadlines can help prevent the feeling of being overwhelmed. It's also important to set aside time for rest and activities that you enjoy.

Maintaining Stress Balance Over Time

Maintaining a healthy balance of stress involves regular self-assessment and adjustment of your stress management techniques. It's important to recognize when your current strategies are no longer effective and to be open to trying new approaches.

Building resilience, as mentioned earlier, is a key part of maintaining stress balance. This includes developing a positive outlook, learning from past experiences, and maintaining a sense of control over your life and choices.

His books, such as Full Catastrophe Living and Wherever You Go, There You Are, have become classics in the field of mindfulness and stress reduction.

Jon Kabat-Zinn's life and work serve as a powerful example of the potential benefits of mindfulness and stress management techniques.

The Role of Mindfulness

Understanding Mindfulness

Mindfulness is the practice of being fully present and engaged in the moment, aware of your thoughts and feelings without judgment. It involves a conscious direction of our awareness away from the automatic pilot mode that we often operate in and moving towards a more observant, deliberate state of mind.

Mindfulness can be practiced through meditation, but it can also be incorporated into daily activities, such as eating, walking, or listening to music. The key is to pay attention to the sensations, thoughts, and emotions that arise in the present moment without getting caught up in them.

Practicing Mindfulness

To practice mindfulness, you can start with simple exercises like mindful breathing, where you focus on the sensation of breath entering and leaving your body. You can also try body scan meditation, which involves paying attention to different parts of your body and the sensations they experience.

Mindfulness can also be practiced informally by bringing a focused attention to everyday activities. This might involve noticing the taste and texture of your food while eating or the feeling of water on your skin during a shower.

Mindfulness and Emotion and Stress Management

Mindfulness is a powerful tool for managing emotions and stress. By becoming more aware of your thoughts and feelings, you can gain perspective and reduce the intensity of emotional reactions. Mindfulness also helps in recognizing the signs of stress early on, allowing you to take proactive steps to manage it.

Studies have shown that regular mindfulness practice can lead to reductions in anxiety and depression, improvements in concentration and memory, and an overall sense of well-being. It can also improve emotional regulation, making it easier to cope with difficult situations.

Case Studies on Managing Emotions and Stress

Real-Life Examples of Managing Emotions and Stress

Case studies provide valuable insights into how individuals manage emotions and stress in real-life situations. For example, a teenager who experiences anxiety before exams might use deep breathing techniques and positive visualization to calm their nerves and improve focus.

Another case study might involve a young person dealing with the stress of moving to a new city. By establishing a routine, seeking out new social connections, and using mindfulness to stay grounded, they can navigate the transition more smoothly.

Activities for Managing Emotions and Stress

Practical Exercises for Managing Emotions and Stress

There are many practical exercises that can help manage emotions and stress. These include relaxation techniques such as progressive muscle relaxation, where you tense and then relax different muscle groups, and guided imagery, where you visualize a peaceful scene or experience.

Other exercises might involve role-playing to practice emotional responses or writing letters to express difficult emotions. Physical activities like sports or dance can also be effective outlets for emotions and stress relief.

Reflective Activities for Emotion and Stress Management

Reflective activities such as journaling can provide a way to process emotions and stress. Writing about your experiences and feelings can help you understand them more clearly and gain insight into your emotional patterns and stress triggers.

Artistic activities like painting or music can also serve as reflective practices, offering a creative outlet for expressing and managing emotions and stress.

Emotion and Stress Management and Self-confidence

How Managing Emotions and Stress Builds Self-Confidence

Successfully managing emotions and stress can lead to increased self-confidence. When you feel in control of your emotional responses and can handle stress effectively, you are more likely to feel confident in your ability to face challenges and navigate complex situations.

This sense of self-efficacy can encourage you to take on new opportunities and step out of your comfort zone, knowing that you have the skills to cope with whatever emotions and stress may arise.

The Interplay Between Self-Confidence and

Emotion and Stress Management

Self-confidence and emotion and stress management are closely linked. As you become more confident in your abilities, you may find it easier to manage your emotions and stress. Conversely, as you develop better emotion and stress management techniques, your self-confidence is likely to grow.

This positive feedback loop can lead to a virtuous cycle of personal growth and mastery, where improvements in one area reinforce and enhance the other.

Further Reading

If you're interested in exploring more about the interplay between self-confidence and emotion and stress management, here are some recommended books and resources:

1. "The Confidence Code for Girls: Taking Risks, Messing Up, and Becoming Your Amazingly Imperfect, Totally Powerful Self" by Katty Kay and Claire Shipman. This book is a great guide for teenagers, especially girls, to understand and boost their self-confidence.
2. "Mindfulness for Teens: Discovering Your Inner Strength" by Dzung X. Vo. This book introduces mindfulness practices to help

Emotion and Stress Management and Relationships

How Emotion and Stress Management Impact Relationships

Emotion and stress management can have a significant impact on relationships. Being able to manage your own emotions allows for healthier and more constructive interactions with others. It can prevent conflicts from escalating and help you respond to others with empathy and understanding.

Similarly, managing stress effectively can prevent it from spilling over into your relationships. When you are less stressed, you are more likely to be present and attentive in your interactions with others, which can strengthen your relationships.

Managing Emotions and Stress for Healthy Relationships

To foster healthy relationships, it's important to communicate openly about your emotions and stress. This can help prevent misunderstandings and provide an opportunity for mutual support. It's also important to set boundaries and practice self-care, ensuring that you are not taking on too much stress from others.

Developing coping strategies that you can use together, such as going for walks or practicing relaxation techniques, can also help manage emotions and stress within relationships.

Emotion and Stress Management and Goal Achievement

The Role of Emotion and Stress Management in

Achieving Goals

Effective emotion and stress management can play a crucial role in achieving goals. When you are able to stay calm and focused, you are better equipped to plan and execute the steps needed to reach your objectives. Managing stress also helps maintain the motivation and energy required to pursue your goals.

Additionally, understanding and managing your emotions can help you navigate the setbacks and challenges that inevitably arise when working towards a goal. It allows you to maintain a positive outlook and persevere in the face of difficulties.

Managing Emotions and Stress for Goal Achievement

To use emotion and stress management in service of goal achievement, it's important to set realistic expectations and be prepared to adjust your plans as needed. Celebrating small successes along the way can help maintain motivation and reduce stress.

It's also helpful to develop a toolkit of strategies that you can turn to when facing emotional challenges or stress related to your goals. This might include seeking feedback, breaking goals down into manageable tasks, or using visualization techniques to stay focused on the desired outcome.

The Power of Managing Emotions and Stress

Reflecting on the Journey of Managing Emotions and Stress

Reflecting on the journey of managing emotions and stress reveals the profound impact that these skills can have on personal mastery and overall quality of life. By developing the ability to understand and regulate emotions and to cope with stress, individuals can enhance their mental, emotional, and physical well-being.

This journey is not always easy, and it requires continuous effort and self-reflection. However, the rewards of greater self-awareness, improved relationships, and the ability to achieve one's goals make it a worthwhile endeavor.

Looking Forward: Emotion and Stress Management in the Journey to Mastery

As you continue your journey to personal mastery, remember that emotion and stress management are skills that can be developed and refined over time. They are not static abilities but rather dynamic processes that evolve as you grow and face new challenges.

Embracing the practice of managing emotions and stress will not only help you navigate the complexities of adolescence but will also equip you with valuable tools for the rest of your life. By mastering these skills, you set the foundation for a fulfilling and balanced journey to personal mastery.

1. What is the role of emotions in personal mastery?

    A. Emotions only hinder personal mastery.
    B. Emotions only facilitate personal mastery.
    C. Emotions have no role in personal mastery.
    D. Emotions can either hinder or facilitate personal mastery depending on how they are managed.

2. What is a strategy for managing stress?

A. Ignoring stressors
B. Increasing workload
C. Engaging in physical activity D. Avoiding relaxation

3. How does mindfulness contribute to emotion and stress management?

    A. Mindfulness suppresses emotions.
    B. Mindfulness increases stress levels.
    C. Mindfulness helps in recognizing and accepting emotions and stress, which is a step towards managing them.
    D. Mindfulness has no contribution to emotion and stress management.

4. How does managing emotions and stress impact relationships?

    A. It leads to isolation and loneliness.
    B. It can lead to healthier relationships as it allows for better communication and understanding.
    C. It has no impact on relationships.
    D. It makes relationships more stressful.

5. What is the role of emotion and stress management in achieving goals?

    A. Emotion and stress management can hinder goal achievement.
    B. Emotion and stress management can facilitate goal achievement by promoting focus, resilience, and motivation.
    C. Emotion and stress management has no role in achieving goals.
    D. Emotion and stress management only facilitates goal achievement if the goal is related to emotion or stress.

8. CULTIVATING RESILIENCE

Understanding Resilience

What is Resilience?

Resilience is the capacity to recover quickly from difficulties; it's about bouncing back from challenges and setbacks. It involves enduring the stress and adversity that life throws your way and emerging from these experiences stronger and more capable. Resilience is not an innate trait that people either have or do not have; it involves behaviors, thoughts, and actions that can be learned and developed by anyone.

A resilient individual displays endurance in the face of difficulty and the ability to adapt to changing circumstances. This adaptability is crucial, as it allows one to navigate through life's inevitable ups and downs with grace and determination. Resilience is often compared to a rubber band, which can stretch under pressure but returns to its original shape once the pressure is released. Similarly, resilient people can withstand stress without breaking and return to their pre-stress state of well-being.

The Role of Resilience in Personal Mastery

In the journey to personal mastery, resilience plays a pivotal role. It is the foundation upon which personal growth and self-improvement are built. When you are resilient, you are better equipped to handle the challenges that come with setting and pursuing goals. You are also more likely to persevere in the face of setbacks and continue working towards your objectives.

Resilience contributes to personal mastery by fostering a mindset that views challenges as opportunities for growth. It encourages a proactive approach to learning and self-development. By cultivating resilience, individuals can maintain focus on their long-term vision, even when immediate circumstances are discouraging. This ability to stay the course is essential for anyone seeking to achieve their full potential.

The Importance of Resilience

Benefits of Resilience

The benefits of resilience are manifold. Resilient individuals tend to lead happier and more fulfilling lives. They can manage stress more effectively and are less likely to experience feelings of helplessness or hopelessness. Resilience also contributes to better mental health, as it is associated with lower rates of depression and anxiety.

Moreover, resilience has physical health benefits. It can lead to better cardiovascular health and a stronger immune system, as resilient individuals are less affected by the physical manifestations of stress. In the social realm, resilience allows people to build and maintain healthier relationships. It equips them with the emotional intelligence to navigate interpersonal conflicts and to provide and seek support when needed.

Resilience and Personal Growth

Personal growth is deeply intertwined with resilience. As individuals encounter and overcome obstacles, they gain insight into their capabilities and limitations. This self-awareness is a key component of personal development. Resilience also encourages a growth mindset, which is the belief that abilities and intelligence can be developed through dedication and hard work.

Through resilience, individuals learn to embrace challenges as catalysts for growth rather than as insurmountable barriers. This perspective allows them to stretch beyond their comfort zones and to undertake new and rewarding experiences. As a result, they grow not only in skill and knowledge but also in character and self-assurance.

Building Resilience

Strategies for Building Resilience

Building resilience is a proactive process that involves several strategies. One key strategy is to foster strong, supportive relationships with family and friends. These relationships provide emotional support and a sense of belonging, which are critical during tough times. Another strategy is to develop good communication skills, which enable individuals to express their needs and to seek help when necessary.

Cultivating a positive view of oneself is also important. This involves recognizing one's strengths and accomplishments and using positive self-talk to build self-esteem. Additionally, learning to manage strong feelings and impulses is a crucial part of building resilience. This can be achieved through techniques such as mindfulness, which helps individuals stay grounded in the present moment and respond to situations with clarity and calmness.

Practicing Resilience-Building Activities

There are many activities that can help build resilience. Regular physical exercise, for example, not only improves physical health but also reduces stress and enhances mood. Engaging in hobbies and interests can provide a sense of accomplishment and joy, which are vital for resilience. Volunteering or helping others can also foster resilience by providing a sense of purpose and community.

Another effective activity is to set realistic goals and to take small steps towards achieving them. This approach helps build confidence and a sense of control over one's life. Practicing gratitude is another activity that can enhance resilience. By focusing on what is positive in one's life, individuals can maintain an optimistic outlook even in the face of adversity.

Maintaining Resilience Over Time

Maintaining resilience over time requires continuous effort and self-reflection. It involves recognizing when one's resilience is being tested and actively using coping strategies to deal with stress. It also means being willing to adapt and change strategies as circumstances evolve.

Self-care is an essential part of maintaining resilience. This includes getting enough sleep, eating a balanced diet, and taking time to relax and recharge. It is also important to keep learning and growing, as personal development contributes to a resilient mindset. Finally, maintaining a hopeful outlook is key. By visualizing what is possible and remaining focused on long-term goals, individuals can sustain their resilience through life's challenges.

Overcoming Resilience Challenges

Identifying Resilience Challenges

Overcoming resilience challenges begins with identifying them. Common challenges include experiencing a significant loss, facing persistent stress, or dealing with a sudden change. It is important to acknowledge these challenges and to understand how they affect one's emotions and behaviors.

Self-awareness is crucial in this process. By being mindful of one's thoughts and feelings, individuals can recognize patterns that may indicate a dip in resilience, such as negative self-talk or withdrawal from social activities. Identifying these signs early on can help in addressing the challenges more effectively.

Strategies for Overcoming Resilience Challenges

Once resilience challenges are identified, there are several strategies to overcome them. One effective approach is to reframe negative thoughts into positive ones. This cognitive restructuring can shift one's perspective and reduce the impact of stress. Another strategy is to focus on what can be controlled and to let go of what cannot. This helps reduce feelings of helplessness and empowers individuals to act where possible.

Building a strong support network is also a key strategy. Friends, family, and professionals can offer guidance, encouragement, and different perspectives on the challenges being faced. Additionally, practicing stress reduction techniques such as deep breathing, meditation, or yoga can help manage the physical and emotional effects of stress.

Seeking Support for Resilience Challenges

Seeking support is a vital part of overcoming resilience challenges. This support can come from various sources, including mental health professionals, support groups, or community organizations. These resources can provide valuable tools and strategies for building and maintaining resilience.

It is important to remember that seeking help is a sign of strength, not weakness. By reaching out, individuals demonstrate their commitment to personal growth and their willingness to take proactive steps towards overcoming their challenges.

Did You Know?

Resilience is not just about overcoming adversity. It's also about learning from the experience and growing stronger as a result. This process is often referred to as "post-traumatic growth".

Post-traumatic growth can lead to improved relationships, increased sense of personal strength, changed priorities, and a richer appreciation of life.

Studies have shown that resilience can be learned and developed. It's not something you're either born with or without.

Resilience is like a muscle. The more you use it, the stronger it gets.

The Role of Positive Mindset

Understanding Positive Mindset

A positive mindset is a mental and emotional attitude that focuses on the bright side of life and expects positive results. It is not about ignoring life's difficulties, but rather about approaching them with optimism and confidence. A positive mindset involves recognizing that setbacks are temporary and that one has the skills and abilities to overcome them.

This mindset is characterized by positive thinking, which involves the practice of focusing on the good in any given situation. It also includes the ability to see opportunities in challenges and to learn from mistakes. A positive mindset contributes to resilience by providing a hopeful and constructive approach to life's challenges.

Cultivating a Positive Mindset

Cultivating a positive mindset can be achieved through various practices. One is to practice gratitude by regularly reflecting on and appreciating the good things in life. Another is to surround oneself with positive influences, such as uplifting books, media, and people who encourage and inspire.

Setting and achieving goals, no matter how small, can also contribute to a positive mindset. Each accomplishment reinforces the belief in one's abilities and fosters a sense of progress. Additionally, engaging in positive self-talk and challenging negative beliefs about oneself can shift one's perspective towards a more positive outlook.

Positive Mindset and Resilience

A positive mindset is a cornerstone of resilience. It enables individuals to cope with stress and recover from setbacks more effectively. By maintaining a positive outlook, resilient people can stay motivated and continue to work towards their goals, even in the face of adversity.

Furthermore, a positive mindset encourages a proactive approach to problem-solving and decision-making. It allows individuals to see beyond the immediate obstacles and to envision a successful outcome. This forward-thinking attitude is essential for building and sustaining resilience.

Case Studies on Building Resilience
Real-Life Examples of Building Resilience

There are countless real-life examples of individuals who have demonstrated remarkable resilience. One such example is the story of Malala Yousafzai, who, after surviving an assassination attempt by the Taliban, became a global advocate for girls' education. Her resilience in the face of life-threatening adversity and her continued activism inspires people around the world.

Another example is the life of Nelson Mandela, who spent 27 years in prison for his fight against apartheid in South Africa. Despite the harsh conditions and long-term imprisonment, Mandela emerged as a leader who would go on to become the country's president and a symbol of reconciliation and peace.

Lessons Learned from Case Studies

The lessons learned from these case studies are powerful. They show that resilience can be developed in the face of extreme hardship and that it can lead to extraordinary achievements. These stories teach us that resilience is not just about surviving but also about thriving and making a positive impact on the world.

They also highlight the importance of having a purpose and staying committed to one's values. Both Malala and Mandela had a clear vision and a deep sense of mission, which fueled their resilience. Their experiences remind us that with determination and a strong sense of purpose, individuals can overcome even the most daunting challenges.

> What are your core values? What is your purpose in life? How do these guide your actions and decisions, especially during challenging times?
>
> Learning from Role Models:
>
> Think about the stories of Malala and Mandela. How did their sense of purpose contribute to their resilience? Can you think of other role models who have shown resilience in the face of adversity? What can you learn from them?

Applying Lessons Learned:

How can you apply the lessons learned from these case studies in your own life? How can you cultivate resilience and use it to not just survive, but thrive and make a positive impact?

Activities for Building Resilience

Practical Exercises for Building Resilience

There are many practical exercises that can help build resilience.
Journaling, for instance, is a powerful tool for self-reflection and for processing emotions. Writing about experiences and feelings can provide clarity and can help individuals work through challenges.

Another exercise is to create a resilience plan that outlines strategies for coping with stress and adversity. This plan can include techniques such as mindfulness, exercise, and reaching out to support networks. Role-playing scenarios that require resilience can also be beneficial, as it allows individuals to practice their responses to difficult situations in a safe environment.

Reflective Activities for Building Resilience

Reflective activities are also important for building resilience. These can include meditation, which helps individuals gain perspective and stay centered during stressful times. Reflecting on past successes and the strategies used to achieve them can also reinforce resilience by reminding individuals of their strengths and abilities.

Additionally, setting aside time for self-reflection can help individuals align their actions with their values and goals.

This alignment is crucial for maintaining motivation and for making progress in the face of obstacles.

Further Reading

Interested in learning more about resilience and self-improvement? Here are some recommended books that can help you deepen your understanding:

1. "The Resilience Factor: 7 Keys to Finding Your Inner Strength and Overcoming Life's Hurdles" by Karen Reivich and Andrew Shatte. This book offers practical advice and strategies for building resilience.

2. "Mindset: The New Psychology of Success" by Carol S. Dweck. This book explores the concept of "mindset" and how our beliefs about our abilities can impact our success.

3. "The Power of Now: A Guide to Spiritual Enlightenment" by Eckhart Tolle. This book provides insights into the practice of mindfulness and living in the present moment, which can help in building resilience.

4. "The 7 Habits of Highly Effective Teens" by Sean Covey. This book is a teenager-friendly guide to developing habits that foster success and resilience.

Remember, the journey of self-improvement is a lifelong process. Keep exploring, learning, and growing!

Resilience and Self-Confidence

How Building Resilience Builds Self-Confidence

Building resilience has a direct impact on self-confidence. As individuals overcome challenges and develop coping strategies, they gain a sense of mastery over their lives. This sense of mastery boosts self-confidence, as it demonstrates to individuals that they are capable of handling life's difficulties.

Furthermore, each time a person successfully navigates a challenging situation, their belief in their own abilities grows. This accumulated experience of overcoming adversity contributes to a robust self-confidence that can be applied to future challenges.

The Interplay Between Self-Confidence and Resilience

The relationship between self-confidence and resilience is reciprocal. While building resilience enhances self-confidence, having self-confidence also contributes to resilience. When individuals believe in their abilities, they are more likely to take on challenges and to persist in the face of setbacks.

Self-confident individuals are also more likely to seek out and utilize resources that can help them cope with adversity. This proactive approach to problem-solving is a key aspect of resilience. Therefore, fostering self-confidence is an important part of cultivating resilience.

Resilience and Relationships

How Resilience Impacts Relationships

Resilience has a significant impact on relationships. Resilient individuals are better equipped to handle the stresses and strains that can occur in relationships. They are more likely to communicate effectively, to show empathy, and to work through conflicts constructively.

Additionally, resilience allows individuals to be supportive partners during challenging times. By maintaining their own emotional balance, they can provide stability and comfort to others. This support can strengthen the bond between individuals and can foster deeper, more meaningful connections.

Building Resilience for Healthy Relationships

Building resilience can contribute to the development of healthy relationships. It involves learning to set healthy boundaries, to express needs and concerns openly, and to listen actively to others. It also includes the ability to forgive and to move past grievances, which is essential for long-term relationship satisfaction.

By cultivating resilience, individuals can approach relationships with a positive and flexible mindset. They can adapt to changes within the relationship and can work together with their partners to overcome challenges. This collaborative approach is key to building and maintaining healthy relationships.

Resilience and Goal Achievement

The Role of Resilience in Achieving Goals

Resilience plays a crucial role in achieving goals. It enables individuals to stay focused and motivated, even when progress is slow or when obstacles arise. Resilient individuals are more likely to view setbacks as temporary and as opportunities to learn and grow, rather than as reasons to give up.

This tenacity and perseverance are essential for goal achievement. By maintaining a resilient mindset, individuals can continue to take steps towards their goals, adjusting their strategies as needed and remaining committed to their vision.

Building Resilience for Goal Achievement

Building resilience for goal achievement involves setting clear and realistic goals, breaking them down into manageable steps, and celebrating small victories along the way. It also involves developing a support system that can provide encouragement and advice.

Additionally, maintaining a positive attitude and staying flexible in the face of change can help individuals navigate the path to their goals. By cultivating resilience, they can maintain the momentum needed to achieve their objectives and to overcome any barriers that stand in their way.

The Power of Resilience

Reflecting on the Journey of Building Resilience

Reflecting on the journey of building resilience reveals its transformative power. Through the process of facing and overcoming adversity, individuals learn about themselves and their capabilities. They develop a deeper understanding of their values, strengths, and areas for growth.

This journey is not always easy, but it is always worthwhile. The skills and insights gained through building resilience are invaluable and can be applied to all areas of life. They contribute to a sense of empowerment and a belief in one's ability to shape one's own destiny.

Looking Forward: Resilience in the Journey to Mastery

Looking forward, resilience will continue to be a key component in the journey to personal mastery. As individuals encounter new challenges and opportunities, their resilience will enable them to adapt, grow, and thrive.

The journey to mastery is a lifelong process, and resilience is the companion that makes this journey possible. By continuing to cultivate resilience, individuals can look forward to a future filled with growth, achievement, and personal fulfillment.

9. NURTURING RELATIONSHIPS

Understanding Relationships

What is a Relationship?

A relationship is a connection or bond between two or more people. These connections can be based on emotions, social commitments, interactions, or legal obligations. Relationships are a fundamental aspect of human life and can vary in duration and significance. They are formed through a series of interactions and can be influenced by individual behaviors, communication, and shared experiences.

Relationships are not static; they evolve over time and require effort from all parties involved to grow and thrive. They can provide support, joy, and companionship, but they can also lead to challenges and conflicts that need to be managed. Understanding the dynamics of relationships is crucial for personal development and well-being.

Types of Relationships

There are various types of relationships that individuals can experience throughout their lives. These include, but are not limited to, family relationships, friendships, romantic relationships, professional relationships, and acquaintances.

Each type of relationship serves a different purpose and brings unique benefits and challenges.

- Family relationships are often characterized by a deep emotional bond and a sense of obligation or duty.

- Friendships are formed based on mutual interests, support, and enjoyment of each other's company.

- Romantic relationships involve emotional and often physical intimacy, and they require a high level of commitment and communication.

- Professional relationships are built on mutual respect and common goals within the workplace or industry.

- Acquaintances are individuals we know but with whom we have a limited and often formal relationship.

Recognizing the different types of relationships can help individuals understand the expectations and boundaries associated with each, leading to healthier interactions and connections.

The Role of Relationships in Personal Mastery

Relationships play a significant role in personal mastery, which is the ongoing process of self-improvement and self-understanding. Healthy relationships can provide support, feedback, and a sense of belonging, all of which are essential for personal growth. They can also challenge us to develop better communication skills, empathy, and patience.

In the journey towards personal mastery, relationships act as mirrors, reflecting our strengths and areas for improvement. They encourage us to set goals, make positive changes, and become more resilient. By nurturing relationships, we not only enhance our connections with others but also foster our own development and self-discovery.

The Importance of Healthy Relationships

Benefits of Healthy Relationships

Healthy relationships are essential for our mental and emotional wellbeing. They provide a source of comfort, reduce stress, and contribute to our overall happiness. When we have strong, positive relationships, we are more likely to feel confident and supported in our endeavors. These relationships can also improve our physical health by encouraging healthier lifestyle choices and providing a network of care during times of illness or distress.

Furthermore, healthy relationships can lead to increased longevity, as social connections have been linked to a lower risk of premature death. They also offer opportunities for personal growth, as we learn from the diverse perspectives and experiences of those we are close to.

Healthy Relationships and Personal Growth

Personal growth is greatly influenced by the quality of our relationships. Healthy relationships encourage us to step out of our comfort zones, try new things, and develop new skills. They provide a safe space for us to express our thoughts and feelings, which is crucial for self-awareness and emotional intelligence.

In a healthy relationship, individuals are able to give and receive constructive feedback, which is invaluable for personal development. These relationships also foster a sense of accountability, motivating us to follow through on our commitments and strive for continuous improvement.

1. A study by the Harvard Business Review found that constructive feedback can improve performance by up

to 39%.

2. According to a survey by the Society for Human Resource Management, 72% of employees think their performance would improve if their managers would provide corrective feedback.

Building Healthy Relationships

Identifying Characteristics of Healthy Relationships

Healthy relationships are characterized by a number of key attributes. These include mutual respect, trust, honesty, support, fairness, separate identities, and good communication. Recognizing these characteristics can help individuals understand what to strive for in their own relationships.

Mutual respect involves valuing each other's opinions and feelings, while trust is the foundation that allows individuals to feel secure and confident in the relationship. Honesty is crucial for building trust and maintaining open communication. Support means being there for each other during both good times and bad. Fairness ensures that both parties contribute to the relationship and that one person does not bear an unfair share of responsibilities. Separate identities mean that each person retains their individuality and does not lose themselves in the relationship. Lastly, good communication is the tool that allows all these characteristics to function effectively.

Steps to Building Healthy Relationships

Building healthy relationships involves several steps that require intention and effort. The first step is to understand yourself and your expectations for the relationship. Next, it is important to communicate openly and honestly with the other person, expressing your thoughts and feelings while also listening to theirs.

Another key step is to establish boundaries, which helps to ensure that both parties feel comfortable and respected. It is also crucial to show appreciation and acknowledge the positive aspects of the relationship. Lastly, working through conflicts in a constructive manner is essential for the longevity and health of the relationship.

Maintaining Healthy Relationships Over Time

Maintaining healthy relationships over time requires ongoing attention and care. It involves regular check-ins with each other to discuss the state of the relationship and address any concerns. It also means continuing to show appreciation and celebrating achievements together.

Another important aspect of maintenance is adapting to changes, as individuals and relationships evolve. This may involve renegotiating boundaries or finding new ways to connect. Additionally, investing time and energy into the relationship is crucial, as is the willingness to seek help when needed, whether from friends, family, or professionals.

Overcoming Relationship Challenges

Identifying Relationship Challenges

Challenges in relationships can arise from a variety of sources, including communication breakdowns, trust issues, differing values or goals, and external pressures such as stress from work or family obligations. It is important to identify these challenges early on to address them effectively.

Some common signs of relationship challenges include

frequent arguments, feelings of resentment, emotional distance, and a lack of mutual support. Recognizing these signs can help individuals take proactive steps to improve the health of their relationships.

Strategies for Overcoming Relationship Challenges

Overcoming relationship challenges often requires a combination of strategies. One effective approach is to improve communication by practicing active listening and expressing oneself clearly and respectfully. Another strategy is to build trust through consistent actions and reliability.

It is also helpful to focus on problem-solving rather than placing blame, and to seek common ground when dealing with differences. Additionally, making time for each other and engaging in shared activities can strengthen the bond and create positive experiences.

Seeking Support for Relationship Challenges

Sometimes, relationship challenges can be difficult to overcome without outside help. Seeking support from trusted friends, family members, or professionals such as counselors or therapists can provide new perspectives and strategies for improvement.

Support groups and workshops can also be valuable resources, offering a space to learn from others who may be facing similar issues. It is important to remember that seeking help is a sign of strength and a commitment to the health of the relationship.

The Role of Communication

Understanding Communication

Communication is the process of sharing information, thoughts, and feelings between people. Effective communication is a two-way street that involves both expressing oneself and listening to others. It is the cornerstone of healthy relationships and is essential for understanding and being understood.

There are many forms of communication, including verbal, non-verbal, written, and digital. Each form has its own nuances and requires different skills to be used effectively. Understanding the various forms of communication and when to use them can greatly enhance the quality of relationships.

Practicing Effective Communication

Practicing effective communication involves several key components. It is important to speak clearly and directly, using "I" statements to express personal feelings without blaming others. Active listening is another crucial skill, which means fully concentrating on the speaker, understanding their message, and responding thoughtfully.

Non-verbal cues such as body language, eye contact, and tone of voice also play a significant role in communication. Being aware of these cues and ensuring they match the verbal message can prevent misunderstandings. Additionally, being open to feedback and willing to adjust communication styles can lead to more meaningful interactions.

Communication and Relationships

Communication is the lifeblood of relationships. It allows individuals to share their needs, desires, and concerns with each other, fostering a deeper understanding and connection. When communication breaks down, it can lead to conflicts and a weakening of the relationship.

On the other hand, strong communication skills can help resolve conflicts, build trust, and strengthen the bond between individuals. By prioritizing effective communication, relationships can become more resilient and fulfilling.

> Active listening: Communication is not just about speaking, but also about listening. Active listening involves fully focusing on, understanding, and responding to the speaker, rather than just passively 'hearing' the message.
>
> Emotional intelligence: Effective communication often requires emotional intelligence, which is the ability to understand and manage your own emotions, and those of the people around you.

So, next time you're in a conversation, remember that there's more to communication than just words!

Case Studies on Nurturing Relationships

Real-Life Examples of Nurturing Relationships

There are many real-life examples of individuals and communities that have successfully nurtured relationships. These case studies often highlight the importance of empathy, understanding, and a willingness to work through difficulties.

For instance, a study of long-term friendships revealed that consistent communication, shared experiences, and mutual support were key factors in maintaining the relationship over time. Another case study of a successful mentor-mentee relationship showed that setting clear expectations, providing constructive feedback, and celebrating achievements together contributed to a strong and beneficial connection.

Lessons Learned from Case Studies

The lessons learned from these case studies can be applied to various types of relationships. They demonstrate that nurturing relationships requires effort, patience, and a commitment to growth. Additionally, they show that challenges can be overcome with the right strategies and support.

These case studies also emphasize the value of diversity in relationships, as different perspectives can lead to richer experiences and learning opportunities. They remind us that every relationship is unique and that there is no one-size-fits-all approach to nurturing them.

Activities for Nurturing Relationships

Practical Exercises for Nurturing Relationships

There are many practical exercises that can help individuals nurture their relationships. These include activities such as regular check-ins to discuss the state of the relationship, setting shared goals, and participating in activities that both parties enjoy.

Other exercises include practicing gratitude by acknowledging what one appreciates about the other person, and engaging in trust-building activities such as sharing personal stories or fears. These exercises can strengthen the bond and improve the overall health of the relationship.

Reflective Activities for Nurturing Relationships

Reflective activities are also important for nurturing relationships. These can include journaling about the relationship, reflecting on past successes and challenges, and considering ways to improve the connection moving forward.

Additionally, taking time to understand each other's love

languages or communication styles can lead to greater empathy and a more tailored approach to nurturing the relationship. Reflective activities encourage mindfulness and intentionality in relationships.

Relationships and Self-Confidence

How Nurturing Relationships Builds Self-Confidence

Nurturing relationships can have a profound impact on self-confidence. When individuals feel supported and valued in their relationships, they are more likely to take risks and pursue their goals. This sense of security can boost self-esteem and encourage personal growth.

Positive feedback and encouragement from others can also reinforce one's self-worth and abilities. Furthermore, healthy relationships provide a safety net for when things don't go as planned, allowing individuals to bounce back with greater resilience.

The Interplay Between Self-Confidence and Relationships

The relationship between self-confidence and relationships is reciprocal. While nurturing relationships can build self-confidence, having selfconfidence can also lead to healthier relationships. Confident individuals are more likely to set boundaries, communicate effectively, and contribute positively to their relationships.

Self-confidence allows individuals to be authentic and true to themselves, which is attractive to others and can lead to more genuine and fulfilling connections. It also enables individuals to handle relationship challenges with grace and composure.

Further Reading

Want to delve deeper into the world of self-confidence and relationships? Here are some recommended books that can help you understand and develop these areas further:

1. "The Six Pillars of Self-Esteem" by Nathaniel Branden: This book explores the importance of self-esteem in our lives and offers practical advice on how to improve it.

2. "Daring Greatly: How the Courage to Be Vulnerable Transforms the Way We Live, Love, Parent, and Lead" by Brené Brown: This book discusses the concept of vulnerability and its role in building strong relationships and self-confidence. The book was actually my inspiration for my TEDx talk on Vulnerability.

3. "The Gifts of Imperfection: Let Go of Who You Think You're Supposed to Be and Embrace Who You Are" by Brené Brown: This book encourages readers to embrace their imperfections and live a more authentic life.

4. "The Confidence Code: The Science and Art of Self-Assurance What Women Should Know" by Katty Kay and Claire Shipman: This book explores the concept of confidence, its importance, and how to build it.

Remember, reading is just the first step. Applying what you learn to your daily life is what truly makes a difference. Happy reading!

Relationships and Goal Achievement

The Role of Relationships in Achieving Goals

Relationships can play a crucial role in achieving personal and professional goals. Having a supportive network can provide motivation, advice, and resources that are invaluable in the pursuit of one's objectives.
Relationships can also hold individuals accountable, keeping them on track and focused on their goals.

Collaborative goals, such as those set by teams or partners, can foster a sense of unity and shared purpose, leading to greater success. The encouragement and feedback received from others can also help refine goals and strategies for achieving them.

Nurturing Relationships for Goal Achievement

Nurturing relationships for goal achievement involves recognizing the contributions of others and working together towards common objectives.
It requires clear communication about goals, expectations, and progress.

Celebrating milestones and successes together can strengthen the relationship and reinforce commitment to shared goals.

It is also important to be supportive of each other's individual goals, offering assistance and understanding when needed. By aligning relationship dynamics with goal achievement, individuals can create a powerful synergy that benefits all parties involved.

The Power of Nurturing Relationships

Reflecting on the Journey of Nurturing

Relationships

Reflecting on the journey of nurturing relationships reveals the many ways in which they enrich our lives. Relationships provide companionship, support, and joy, and they challenge us to grow and become better versions of ourselves. The effort invested in nurturing relationships is rewarded with deeper connections and a stronger sense of community.

The journey also teaches us about the importance of empathy, patience, and communication. It highlights the need for continuous effort and the value of overcoming challenges together. Each relationship is a learning experience that contributes to our personal mastery.

Looking Forward: Relationships in the Journey to Mastery

Looking forward, relationships will continue to play a vital role in the journey to personal mastery. As individuals grow and evolve, so too will their relationships. The skills and insights gained from nurturing relationships will serve as a foundation for future interactions and personal development.

Embracing the power of relationships means recognizing their potential to transform lives. It involves committing to the ongoing process of building and maintaining healthy connections with others. By doing so, individuals can create a supportive network that will accompany them on their journey to mastery.

1. What is one of the benefits of healthy relationships?

    A. They increase stress levels
    B. They contribute to personal growth
    C. They limit personal freedom
    D. They discourage self-improvement

2. What is a key characteristic of a healthy relationship?

    A. Constant conflict
    B. Lack of communication
    C. Mutual respect
    D. One-sided decision making

3. What is a common challenge in relationships?

    A.   Excessive respect
    B.   Overwhelming support
    C. Poor communication
    D. Too much understanding

10. COMMUNICATING EFFECTIVELY

Understanding Communication

What is Communication?

Communication is the process of sharing information, thoughts, and feelings between people through speaking, writing, or body language. Effective communication extends beyond just exchanging information; it is about understanding the emotion and intentions behind the information. It involves a sender transmitting an idea, information, or feeling to a receiver. Successful communication occurs when the receiver comprehends the message as the sender intended.

This process is fundamental to personal mastery because it enables individuals to express themselves, understand others, and build relationships. It is a critical life skill that can determine success in many areas, such as personal relationships and academic and professional settings.

Types of Communication

There are several types of communication, including verbal, non-verbal, written, and visual:

- Verbal Communication: Involves the use of words to

convey a message. This can be in-person, over the phone, via video conferencing, or any other medium where speech is used to communicate.

- Non-verbal Communication: Includes body language, facial expressions, gestures, posture, and eye contact. It can convey a great deal of information without a single word being spoken.

- Written Communication: Involves any message that is transmitted through the written word. This includes letters, emails, texts, social media posts, and more.

- Visual Communication: Involves the use of visual elements, such as art, drawings, sketches, charts, and graphs, to convey ideas and information.

Each type of communication has its own nuances and is important in different contexts. The ability to effectively use and interpret these types of communication is essential for personal mastery.

The Role of Communication in Personal Mastery

Communication plays a pivotal role in personal mastery, as it is the bridge that connects individuals to the world around them. It allows for the expression of thoughts, emotions, and needs, and it facilitates understanding and collaboration with others. Effective communication can lead to improved relationships, better problem-solving, and greater influence in social and professional circles.

Personal mastery involves self-awareness, and communication is a tool for reflecting on and sharing one's inner world. It also requires the ability to listen and understand others' perspectives, which is a key component of effective communication. Mastery of communication skills can lead to a more fulfilling and successful life.

The Importance of Effective Communication

Benefits of Effective Communication

Effective communication offers numerous benefits. It can improve teamwork, enhance decision-making, and promote problem-solving. When people communicate effectively, they are more likely to build rapport and trust. This can lead to better outcomes in negotiations, conflict resolution, and in building and maintaining personal and professional relationships.

Additionally, effective communication can increase efficiency in more practical aspects of life. It can prevent misunderstandings and the need for rework, saving time and resources. It also empowers individuals to express their needs and desires clearly, leading to greater satisfaction and fulfillment.

Effective Communication and Personal Growth

Personal growth is deeply connected to effective communication. As individuals learn to express themselves more clearly and listen to others, they gain deeper insights into their own behaviors and thought patterns.
This self-awareness is a critical step in personal development.

Furthermore, effective communication skills can lead to increased opportunities for learning and advancement. Whether in an educational setting, the workplace, or personal relationships, the ability to convey information clearly and understand others can open doors to new experiences and knowledge.

Quick Facts & Statistics

Communication and Personal Growth

93% of communication is nonverbal, according to research by Dr. Albert Mehrabian. This includes facial expressions, body language, and tone of voice.

Studies show that effective communicators are more likely to be successful in both their personal and professional lives.

According to a survey by the National Association of Colleges and Employers, verbal communication skills are ranked first among a job candidate's 'must have' skills and qualities.

Improving Communication Skills

Research suggests that active listening is a key component of effective communication. It involves fully focusing on, understanding, and responding to a speaker.

Empathy in communication can lead to stronger relationships. It involves understanding and sharing the feelings of another.

Studies show that positive reinforcement, such as praise, can enhance communication by making individuals more likely to share their thoughts and feelings.

Building Effective Communication Skills

Identifying Characteristics of Effective Communication

Effective communication is characterized by clarity, empathy, active listening, and respect. Clarity involves speaking clearly and directly, using language that is understandable to the receiver. Empathy requires putting oneself in the other person's shoes and communicating with sensitivity to their emotions and perspective.

Active listening is another crucial characteristic, involving fully concentrating on what is being said rather than just passively hearing the message. Respect is fundamental, as it involves recognizing the value of others' ideas and feelings and responding appropriately.

Steps to Building Effective Communication Skills

Building effective communication skills involves several steps:

1. Self-Assessment: Begin by understanding your current communication strengths and areas for improvement.

2. Learning: Study the principles of effective communication, including language use, non-verbal cues, and active listening.

3. Practice: Apply these principles in daily interactions and seek feedback from trusted peers or mentors.

4. Reflection: After communicating, take time to reflect on what went well and what could be improved.

5. Adaptation: Be willing to adapt your communication style to different people and situations for the best outcomes.

These steps are iterative and ongoing, as effective

communication is a skill that can always be refined and enhanced.

Maintaining Effective Communication Over Time

To maintain effective communication skills over time, it is important to stay mindful of how you communicate and to continue practicing and refining your skills. This can involve regular self-reflection, continuing education, and staying open to feedback from others.

It is also important to adapt to changing technologies and norms around communication. For example, as digital communication becomes more prevalent, understanding how to effectively convey tone and emotion through text can be crucial.

Overcoming Communication Challenges

Identifying Communication Challenges

Communication challenges can arise from a variety of sources, including cultural differences, personal biases, language barriers, and differing communication styles. Identifying these challenges is the first step toward overcoming them.

It is important to be aware of your own communication habits and to recognize when they may not be effective. Paying attention to the reactions of others can provide valuable clues about how your communication is being received.

Strategies for Overcoming Communication Challenges

Strategies for overcoming communication challenges include:

- Active Listening: Focus on understanding the other person's message before responding.
  - Empathy: Try to understand the other person's perspective and feelings.

- Clarification: Ask questions to clarify understanding and avoid assumptions.

- Adaptation: Adjust your communication style to better fit the other person's preferences.

- Education: Learn about different cultures, languages, and communication norms to broaden your ability to communicate with a diverse range of people.

These strategies can help bridge gaps in understanding and improve the effectiveness of communication.

Seeking Support for Communication Challenges

When facing communication challenges, it can be helpful to seek support from others. This can include mentors, counselors, or communication professionals who can provide guidance and feedback. There are also many resources available, such as books, workshops, and online courses, that can help improve communication skills.

Support groups and practice communities can also be valuable, as they provide a safe space to practice communication and learn from others' experiences.

Online platforms like Coursera and Udemy also offer a variety of communication courses that can be taken at your own pace.

Remember, the key to mastering communication is practice and continuous learning!

The Role of Listening

Understanding Listening

Listening is a critical component of effective communication. It involves not just hearing the words that another person is saying but also understanding the complete message being conveyed. Listening requires attention, interpretation, and response, and it is an active process that demands engagement.

Good listeners can pick up on both the verbal and non-verbal cues that are part of communication. This skill allows them to respond more thoughtfully and accurately to what is being said.

Practicing Effective Listening

Practicing effective listening involves several techniques:

- Maintaining Eye Contact: This shows the speaker that you are focused and engaged.

- Minimizing Distractions: Eliminate or reduce background noise and interruptions.

- Reflecting and Clarifying: Paraphrase what the speaker has said to ensure understanding and ask clarifying questions.

- Being Patient: Allow the speaker to finish their thoughts without interrupting.

- Showing Empathy: Acknowledge the speaker's feelings and perspectives.

By practicing these techniques, you can become a better listener and communicator.

Some will advise that you nod when listening to someone. The reality is that when you do this too often, studies have shown that you will be perceived as being less engaged and even, less intelligent than someone who is still.

So the next time someone is speaking to you – remember – be still, and listen.

Listening and Effective Communication

Listening is the foundation of effective communication. When we listen well, we gain a deeper understanding of the other person's perspective, which can help prevent misunderstandings and build stronger relationships. It also signals to the speaker that we value their thoughts and are genuinely interested in what they have to say.

Effective listening can also enhance our ability to influence and persuade others, as it helps us to tailor our messages in a way that resonates with the listener's needs and desires.

Case Studies on Effective Communication

Real-Life Examples of Effective Communication

There are many real-life examples of effective communication making a significant impact. For instance, consider a situation where a misunderstanding between team members leads to conflict. By employing active listening and empathetic speaking, the team can resolve their differences and work together more harmoniously.

Another example might be a student who is struggling in school. Through open communication with teachers and parents, the student can express their challenges, leading to a collaborative effort to find solutions that support the student's learning.

Lessons Learned from Case Studies

Case studies on effective communication teach us several important lessons:

- Communication is a Two-Way Street: It involves both

speaking and listening, and both parties have a role to play in ensuring the message is understood.

- Clarity is Key: Clear, concise communication can prevent misunderstandings.

- Emotions Matter: Recognizing and addressing emotions can improve communication and relationships.

- Adaptability is Important: Being able to adjust your communication style to suit different situations and people is a valuable skill.

These lessons can be applied to improve communication in a variety of contexts.

Did you know:

> Non-verbal Communication: According to research, a significant portion of our communication is non-verbal. This includes facial expressions, body language, and gestures. So, it's not just what you say, but how you say it that matters!
>
> Active Listening: Active listening is a skill that involves not just hearing the words that another person is saying but also understanding and interpreting them in the context of the entire conversation. It's a crucial part of effective communication.
>
> Emotional Intelligence: This is the ability to understand, use, and manage your own emotions in positive ways to relieve stress, communicate effectively, empathize with others, overcome challenges and defuse conflict. High emotional intelligence can lead to better communication and improved relationships.
>
> Adapting Communication Styles: Different situations

and people require different communication styles. For example, the way you talk to a friend may not be appropriate in a formal setting. Being able to adapt your style is a key communication skill.

Remember, effective communication is a skill that can be learned and improved over time. So, keep practicing!

Activities for Building Effective Communication Skills

Practical Exercises for Building Effective Communication Skills

To build effective communication skills, you can engage in practical exercises such as role-playing different scenarios, practicing public speaking, or participating in group discussions. These activities can help you develop the ability to articulate your thoughts clearly and respond appropriately to others.

Another useful exercise is to record yourself speaking and then analyze the recording to identify areas for improvement. This can help you become more aware of your speech patterns, tone, and body language.

Reflective Activities for Building Effective Communication Skills

Reflective activities, such as journaling about your communication experiences or meditating on your communication goals, can also be beneficial. These activities encourage introspection and self-awareness, which are key components of effective communication.

Additionally, seeking feedback from others and reflecting on that feedback can provide valuable insights into how your communication is perceived and how it can be improved.

Effective Communication and Self-confidence

How Effective Communication Builds Self-Confidence

Effective communication can significantly boost self-confidence. When you are able to express yourself clearly and understand others, you feel more in control and less anxious in social situations. This can lead to a positive feedback loop where successful interactions increase your confidence, which in turn improves your communication skills.

Additionally, being a good communicator can lead to positive recognition and reinforcement from others, further enhancing self-esteem and selfworth.

The Interplay Between Self-Confidence and Effective Communication

Self-confidence and effective communication are deeply interconnected.
Confidence can improve your ability to communicate because it reduces fear of judgment and encourages you to share your ideas. Conversely, as your communication skills improve, you'll likely feel more confident in your ability to connect with others and navigate social situations.

This interplay creates a virtuous cycle that can lead to personal growth and mastery in communication.

Famous Quotes

"The most important thing in communication is hearing what isn't said." - Peter Drucker

Drucker, a renowned management consultant, emphasizes the importance of non-verbal cues in communication. This aligns with our discussion on effective communication and self-confidence. Understanding the unsaid can boost your confidence as you become more adept at interpreting others' feelings and intentions.

"We have two ears and one mouth so that we can listen twice as much as we speak." - Epictetus

Epictetus, a Greek philosopher, highlights the importance of listening in communication. This is a crucial skill in building self-confidence and improving communication. By listening more, we can understand others better, respond more effectively, and build stronger relationships.

"To effectively communicate, we must realize that we are all different in the way we perceive the world and use this understanding as a guide to our communication with others." - Tony Robbins

Robbins, a well-known life coach and motivational speaker, reminds us that understanding others' perspectives is key to effective communication. This understanding can enhance our self-confidence as we become more comfortable navigating diverse viewpoints and social situations.

Effective Communication and Goal Achievement

The Role of Effective Communication in Achieving Goals

Effective communication is essential for achieving goals, whether personal or shared. Clearly articulating your goals to others can help garner support and create accountability. In team settings, effective communication is crucial for coordinating efforts, sharing ideas, and motivating team members.

Additionally, being able to negotiate, persuade, and resolve conflicts through communication can help overcome obstacles that may impede goal achievement.

Building Effective Communication Skills for Goal Achievement

To use communication effectively for goal achievement, it is important to develop a clear message, understand your audience, and convey your message in a way that resonates. Setting specific communication objectives that align with your goals can also help focus your efforts and measure progress.

Practicing assertiveness and learning to ask for what you need are also important communication skills that can aid in achieving your goals.

Conclusion: The Power of Effective Communication

Reflecting on the Journey of Building Effective Communication Skills

Reflecting on the journey of building effective communication skills reveals a path of continuous learning and improvement. It involves developing self-awareness, practicing new skills, adapting to feedback, and growing through experiences.

This journey is not always easy, but the rewards of improved relationships, increased self-confidence, and greater success in achieving goals make it well worth the effort.

Looking Forward: Effective Communication in the Journey to Mastery

Looking forward, effective communication will continue to be a cornerstone of personal mastery. As you encounter new challenges and opportunities, your communication skills will serve as a key tool for navigating the complexities of life.

Embracing the power of effective communication will empower you to connect with others, express your authentic self, and achieve your highest potential.

1. What is one of the benefits of effective communication?

    A. It allows you to control others
    B. It helps in avoiding all conflicts
    C. It eliminates the need for listening
    D. It helps in achieving personal goals

2. Which of the following is NOT a characteristic of effective communication?

    A. Showing empathy
    B. Being clear and concise
    C. Listening actively
    D. Ignoring non-verbal cues

3. How does effective communication contribute to self-

confidence?

    A. It helps you win all arguments
    B. It makes you popular among peers
    C. It allows you to express your thoughts and feelings clearly
    D. It eliminates all self-doubt

4. What is one strategy for overcoming communication challenges?

    A. Speaking louder than the other person
    B. Avoiding difficult conversations
    C. Seeking support and guidance
    D. Ignoring the problem

11. TIME MANAGEMENT AND PRODUCTIVITY

Understanding Time Management

What is Time Management?

Time management is the process of organizing and planning how to divide your time between specific activities. Good time management enables you to work smarter – not harder – so that you get more done in less time, even when time is tight and pressures are high. Failing to manage your time damages your effectiveness and causes stress.

The concept might seem simple, but it involves a range of skills, including planning, setting goals, prioritizing tasks, and monitoring where your time actually goes. It also involves self-awareness and self-regulation to avoid procrastination and maintain productivity. Effective time management requires a shift from activities that are urgent but not necessarily important, to activities that contribute to long-term success and wellbeing.

The Role of Time Management in Personal Mastery

In the context of personal mastery, time management is not

just about getting more tasks completed; it's about aligning your day-to-day actions with your broader life goals. It's a foundational skill that affects all areas of life. By mastering time management, you take control of your life's direction and the pace at which you progress towards your personal vision.

Time management is crucial for personal mastery because it helps you prioritize your development and growth. It ensures that you allocate time to those activities that help you evolve and improve. It also reduces stress by freeing you from the chaos of an unplanned day and the anxiety of missed opportunities.

The Importance of Time Management

Benefits of Time Management

Effective time management comes with a multitude of benefits. It enhances your productivity and efficiency, which can lead to more free time to relax and enjoy hobbies. It can improve your decision-making ability as you have more time to consider options and less pressure to rush judgments. Additionally, it can lead to better work-life balance, ensuring that you have time for both your personal and professional responsibilities.

Another significant benefit is reduced stress levels. When you manage your time well, you're less likely to feel overwhelmed by tasks. This can lead to better mental health and overall well-being. Lastly, good time management can improve your reputation. Being punctual and meeting deadlines shows reliability and respect for others, which can enhance your personal and professional relationships.

Time Management and Personal Growth

Personal growth is about self-improvement and reaching your

full potential. Time management plays a pivotal role in this journey. By effectively managing your time, you create space for learning new skills, reflecting on your experiences, and setting and achieving personal goals. It allows you to focus on activities that align with your values and longterm objectives, rather than getting bogged down by day-to-day distractions.

Moreover, as you become more adept at managing your time, you develop other qualities essential for personal growth, such as discipline, focus, and a proactive mindset. These skills are transferable and will benefit you in all areas of life, from academic success to personal relationships.

Reflect on how time management can aid your personal growth:

1. What is one new skill you would like to learn if you had more time? How can effective time management help you achieve this?

2. How can improved time management enhance your focus and discipline?

3. Think about a recent situation where poor time management affected your performance or results. How could the outcome have been different with better time management?

Building Time Management Skills

Identifying Characteristics of Good Time Management

Good time management is characterized by several key traits. A person with strong time management skills is typically well-organized, with a clear plan for each day. They set realistic goals and break them down into manageable tasks. They prioritize these tasks effectively, focusing on what will have the most significant impact. They are also adaptable, able to adjust their plans as needed without becoming stressed or overwhelmed.

Another characteristic is the ability to set boundaries and say no to nonessential tasks that do not contribute to their goals. Good time managers are also mindful of their habits and routines, recognizing which activities are productive and which are time-wasters. Finally, they regularly review and reflect on their time management practices to continually improve.

Steps to Building Time Management Skills

Building time management skills can be broken down into several steps. The first step is to conduct a time audit to understand where your time currently goes. Next, set clear, measurable goals that align with your values and what you want to achieve. From there, prioritize your tasks using a system like the Eisenhower Matrix, which categorizes tasks by urgency and importance.

Another step is to create a daily schedule or to-do list, allocating specific times for each task. It's also important to anticipate and plan for interruptions and distractions.

Implementing time-blocking techniques can help you focus on one task at a time, and using tools like calendars and timers can keep you on track. Regularly reviewing your progress and adjusting your approach as necessary is the final step to building and refining your time management skills.

Maintaining Time Management Skills Over Time

Maintaining time management skills requires continuous practice and commitment. It's important to stay consistent with the systems and tools that work for you. Regularly revisiting your goals and priorities ensures that your time management efforts are aligned with your personal growth and development.

It's also beneficial to stay flexible and adapt to changing circumstances. Life is unpredictable, and your ability to adjust your time management strategies in the face of new challenges is crucial. Lastly, seek feedback from mentors, peers, or through self-reflection to identify areas for improvement and to celebrate your successes in managing time effectively.

Overcoming Time Management Challenges

Identifying Time Management Challenges

Common time management challenges include procrastination, a lack of clear goals, an inability to prioritize tasks, and constant interruptions. Other challenges might be a tendency to take on too much, a lack of organization, or difficulty in establishing routines. Identifying these challenges is the first step toward overcoming them.

Strategies for Overcoming Time Management Challenges

To overcome time management challenges, start by setting clear, achievable goals. Break larger tasks into smaller, more manageable steps and prioritize them. Develop routines and habits that support your time management goals and learn to set boundaries to minimize interruptions and distractions.

If procrastination is an issue, explore the underlying reasons – are you avoiding a task because it's difficult or unpleasant? Address these feelings and consider using techniques like the Pomodoro Technique to break work into short intervals. Finally, use time management tools like calendars, apps, and to-do lists to stay organized and focused.

Seeking Support for Time Management Challenges

Seeking support can be invaluable in overcoming time management challenges. This could involve working with a mentor or coach who can provide guidance and accountability. Joining a study group or team can also offer motivation and support. Additionally, educational resources such as workshops, books, and online courses can provide strategies and insights to improve your time management skills.

Understanding Productivity

What is Productivity?

Productivity is about the efficiency of your output, whether that's in terms of work, personal projects, or other activities. It's not just about doing more in less time, but also about ensuring that what you do is of high quality and brings you closer to your goals. Productivity involves focusing your efforts on the tasks that have the most significant impact and doing them well.

The Role of Productivity in Time Management

Productivity and time management are closely linked. Effective time management can lead to higher productivity by ensuring that you are working on the right things at the right time. Conversely, being productive can make time management easier because you complete tasks more efficiently, freeing up time for other activities or rest.

Productivity and Time Management

To maximize productivity within your time management framework, it's important to identify your peak productivity periods during the day and schedule your most important tasks for those times. Eliminating distractions and focusing on one task at a time can also boost productivity. Additionally, taking regular breaks using techniques like the Pomodoro Technique can help maintain high levels of productivity throughout the day.

Case Studies on Time Management and Productivity

Real-Life Examples of Time Management and

Productivity

Real-life examples of successful time management and productivity can be found in various fields. For instance, entrepreneurs often must juggle multiple tasks and responsibilities. By using time management techniques such as delegation and prioritization, they can focus on strategic planning and business growth, leading to increased productivity and success.

Lessons Learned from Case Studies

Case studies often reveal that those who are successful in managing their time and being productive share common habits. They tend to be goal oriented, disciplined, and proactive. They also understand the value of rest and recovery in maintaining long-term productivity. These lessons can be applied to your own life to improve your time management and productivity.

> Remember, effective time management is about quality, not quantity.
> It's about working smarter, not harder.

Activities for Building Time Management Skills

Practical Exercises for Building Time Management Skills

Practical exercises for building time management skills include creating a weekly planner, practicing the Eisenhower Matrix for prioritizing tasks, and conducting regular time audits. These exercises help you understand how you currently use your time and how you can improve your time management practices.

Reflective Activities for Building Time Management Skills

Reflective activities such as journaling about your time management experiences, discussing your time management strategies with peers, and setting aside time for regular reviews of your goals and priorities can also be beneficial.

These activities encourage self-awareness and can lead to insights that improve your time management skills.

Time Management, Productivity and Self-confidence

How Time Management and Productivity Builds Self-Confidence

As you become more adept at managing your time and increasing your productivity, you'll likely experience a boost in self-confidence.
Successfully completing tasks and achieving goals reinforces your belief in your abilities. This newfound confidence can then fuel further improvements in time management and productivity, creating a positive feedback loop.

The Interplay Between Self-Confidence, Time Management and Productivity

Self-confidence, time management, and productivity are interrelated. When you manage your time well and are productive, you feel more in control of your life, which enhances your self-confidence. Conversely, having self-confidence can motivate you to take the necessary steps to manage your time better and be more productive.

Test Your Knowledge

How well did you understand the relationship between self-confidence, time management, and productivity? Let's find out!

1. Question 1: How does managing your time well and being productive affect your self-confidence?

2. Question 2: How can self-confidence motivate you to manage your time better and be more productive?

3. Question 3: Can you think of a time when you felt more confident because you were able to manage your time effectively and be productive? Describe the situation.

Reflect on these questions and write down your answers. This will help you understand the concepts better and apply them in your daily life.

Time Management, Productivity and Goal Achievement

The Role of Time Management and Productivity in Achieving Goals

Time management and productivity are critical for achieving goals. By effectively managing your time, you ensure that you are consistently working towards your goals. Productivity ensures that the time you spend is impactful and that you are making progress. Together, they are the engine that drives you towards goal achievement.

Building Time Management Skills for Goal Achievement

To use time management skills for goal achievement, start by aligning your daily tasks with your long-term goals. Use goal-setting frameworks like SMART goals to create actionable plans. Then, apply time management techniques to ensure you are dedicating time to these plans and making steady progress.

The Power of Time Management and Productivity

Reflecting on the Journey of Building Time Management Skills

Reflecting on the journey of building time management skills reveals a path of personal growth and development. As you learn to manage your time better, you gain a deeper understanding of what is truly important to you and how to align your actions with your values and goals.

Looking Forward: Time Management and Productivity in the Journey to Mastery

Looking forward, time management and productivity will continue to play a vital role in your journey to personal mastery. These skills are not static; they evolve as you grow and face new challenges. By continuing to refine your time management and productivity skills, you set yourself up for a lifetime of learning, achievement, and fulfillment.

1. What is Time Management?

    A. The process of building self-confidence and self-esteem.
    B. The process of planning and exercising conscious control of time spent on specific activities.
    C. The process of setting goals and achieving them.
    D. The process of managing stress and emotions.

2. Which of the following is NOT a benefit of good time management?

    A. Better work-life balance
    B. More time for leisure activities
    C. Improved productivity
    D. Increased stress levels

3. What is the relationship between time management and

productivity?

   A. There is no relationship between time management and productivity.
   B. Good time management can lead to increased productivity.
   C. Productivity decreases with good time management.
   D. Productivity and time management are unrelated concepts.

4. Which of the following is a strategy for overcoming time management challenges?

   A. Overloading your schedule
   B. Ignoring the problem
   C. Procrastinating
   D. Setting realistic goals and breaking them down into manageable tasks

5. How does good time management contribute to goal achievement?

   A. It doesn't. Goals can be achieved without good time management.
   B. Good time management allows for more time to be spent on goal-related activities.
   C. Good time management leads to more stress, which motivates goal achievement.
   D. Good time management distracts from goal achievement.

12. EXPLORING PASSIONS AND INTERESTS

Understanding Passions and Interests
What are Passions and Interests?

Passions are the intense, driving feelings that we experience towards activities, subjects, or concepts that hold deep meaning to us. They are the things that we love to do, that energize us, and that we are willing to invest our time and energy into without feeling the weight of obligation. Interests, on the other hand, are the curiosities or preferences we have for certain activities or topics. They are the things that catch our attention and make us want to explore further. While interests can be fleeting or change over time, passions tend to be more enduring and can significantly shape our life choices.

It's important to recognize that passions and interests are not static; they evolve as we grow and gain new experiences. For teenagers, this is a time of exploration and self-discovery, where passions and interests can serve as a compass for future endeavors.

I'd also like to add that anyone who gives you the life advice to solely "follow your passion" has no idea what they're talking about. Each step can lead to you defining what you're passionate about, however you must take those very difficult steps before following your passion can be a viable career choice. You need to know how to manage yourself, your time, your mental state, your physical state, your habits and your goals before your passion will bloom from under you. So don't follow your passion. Follow your routine so you may then explore your passions and interests even more deeply.

The Role of Passions and Interests in Personal Mastery

In the context of personal mastery, passions and interests play a crucial role. They are the fuel that powers our drive to achieve excellence and personal growth. When we align our actions with our passions and interests, we are more likely to engage deeply with our work, persist through challenges, and find joy in the process of learning and growing.

Understanding and embracing our unique passions and interests helps us to carve out a personal path that is both fulfilling and authentic. This alignment is key to developing a sense of purpose and direction in life, which is a cornerstone of personal mastery.

Did You Know?

Passions and interests are not just hobbies or pastimes, they can shape our lives in significant ways. Here are some interesting facts about how passions and interests can impact our lives:

> Boosts Self-Esteem: When we engage in activities that we are passionate about, we tend to feel more confident and competent.
> This can lead to an increase in our self-esteem.

Improves Mental Health: Pursuing our interests can act as a stress reliever and can help improve our overall mental health.

Enhances Social Skills: Many passions and interests involve interacting with others, which can help improve our social skills and make us feel more connected to our community.

Encourages Lifelong Learning: When we are passionate about something, we naturally want to learn more about it. This can foster a love for lifelong learning.

So, don't underestimate the power of your passions and interests.
They can be a driving force in your journey towards personal mastery!

The Importance of Exploring Passions and Interests

Benefits of Exploring Passions and Interests

Exploring passions and interests has numerous benefits. It can lead to increased happiness and life satisfaction, as engaging in activities we love can boost our mood and overall well-being. It also contributes to our sense of identity, helping us understand who we are and what we value most.

Moreover, exploring passions and interests can open doors to new opportunities, whether in education, career, or personal development. It can lead to the discovery of hidden talents and skills and provide a sense of accomplishment when we achieve goals related to our passions.

Exploring Passions and Interests and Personal

Growth

Personal growth is deeply intertwined with the exploration of passions and interests. As we delve into activities that resonate with us, we challenge ourselves, learn new things, and expand our horizons. This process of exploration can lead to greater self-awareness, resilience, and adaptability.

Furthermore, pursuing our passions can teach us valuable life skills such as time management, goal setting, and problem-solving. These skills are transferable and can be applied in various areas of life, contributing to our overall growth and development.

Discovering Your Passions and Interests

Identifying Your Passions and Interests

Identifying your passions and interests can be an exciting journey of self-discovery. Start by reflecting on activities that you enjoy and that make you lose track of time. Consider subjects that you are curious about or that you find yourself researching or talking about often.

It's also helpful to look back on past experiences to identify patterns in the things that have consistently brought you joy or sparked your curiosity. Don't be afraid to explore new areas as well; sometimes, passions and interests are discovered through exposure to something entirely new.

Steps to Discovering Your Passions and Interests

Discovering your passions and interests is a process that involves several steps. First, be open to exploration and trying new things. Join clubs, attend workshops, or volunteer in different fields to gain exposure to a variety of activities and subjects.

Second, pay attention to how you feel during these experiences. Notice what excites you and what feels like a chore. Third, seek feedback from others. Friends, family, and teachers can often provide insights into what they see as your strengths and interests.

Finally, reflect on your experiences. Keep a journal to record your thoughts and feelings about the activities you try. Over time, patterns will emerge that can guide you towards your true passions and interests.

Maintaining Your Passions and Interests Over Time

Maintaining your passions and interests over time requires commitment and effort. Set aside regular time to engage in activities related to your passions, even when life gets busy. Continuously seek out new information and stay current in your areas of interest to keep your passion alive.

It's also important to connect with others who share your passions. Communities, both online and offline, can provide support, inspiration, and opportunities to collaborate. Remember that it's okay for your passions and interests to evolve; allow yourself the flexibility to grow and change.

Overcoming Challenges in Exploring Passions and Interests

Identifying Challenges

Exploring passions and interests is not without its challenges. You may face obstacles such as lack of time, resources, or support. It's important to identify these challenges early on so that you can address them effectively.

Another common challenge is the fear of failure or judgment

from others. This can be particularly daunting when trying something new or pursuing a non-traditional path. Recognizing these fears is the first step towards overcoming them.

Strategies for Overcoming Challenges

To overcome challenges in exploring your passions and interests, start by setting realistic goals and creating a plan to achieve them. Break down larger goals into smaller, manageable tasks to avoid feeling overwhelmed.

Seek out resources that can help you, such as scholarships, mentorship programs, or community groups. Don't be afraid to ask for help or advice from those who have experience in the areas you're interested in.

Finally, cultivate a growth mindset. Embrace challenges as opportunities to learn and grow, rather than as setbacks. This mindset will help you persevere and continue pursuing your passions even when faced with difficulties.

Seeking Support for Challenges

Seeking support is crucial when facing challenges in exploring your passions and interests. Turn to family, friends, teachers, or counselors for encouragement and guidance. They can offer different perspectives and may have resources or connections that can assist you.

Additionally, consider joining online forums or local clubs related to your interests. These communities can provide moral support, advice, and a sense of belonging. Remember, you don't have to navigate these challenges alone; there are many people and resources available to help you.

According to a study by the American Psychological Association, teenagers who pursue their interests have a 34% higher chance of being successful in their careers.

Research from the University of Michigan found that teenagers who actively engage in their interests are more likely to have higher self-esteem and better mental health.

Challenges in Pursuing Passions and Interests

Some interesting statistics:

1. A survey by the National Society for the Gifted and Talented found that 65% of teenagers face challenges in pursuing their passions due to lack of resources or support.

2. According to a study by the Pew Research Center, 58% of teenagers feel pressure to pursue interests that are deemed 'practical' or 'profitable' over their true passions.

Support Systems and Their Impact

Consider these facts:

> Research by the American School Counselor Association shows that teenagers with strong support systems are 70% more likely to overcome challenges in pursuing their interests.

> A study by the Journal of Youth and Adolescence found that online communities can provide significant emotional support and resources for teenagers exploring their interests.

The Role of Passions and Interests in Career Choices

Understanding Career Choices

Career choices are significant decisions that can impact your future. They involve considering your skills, values, and what you want from a job. Understanding how your passions and interests align with potential careers can help you make informed decisions that lead to a fulfilling professional life.

It's important to explore various career options and understand the education or training required for each. This knowledge can help you plan your academic and extracurricular activities to align with your career aspirations.

Passions, Interests and Career Choices

When your career choices are influenced by your passions and interests, you are more likely to find satisfaction and success in your work. You'll be motivated to excel and to continue learning and growing within your field.

Consider how your passions can translate into a career. For example, if you're passionate about art, careers in design, curation, or art education might be a good fit. If you're interested in helping others, consider fields like healthcare, social work, or education.

Exploring Career Choices Based on Passions and Interests

To explore career choices based on your passions and interests, start by researching industries and roles that align with what you love. Informational interviews with professionals in those fields can provide valuable insights.

Internships, part-time jobs, or volunteer work can also give you hands-on experience and help you determine if a particular career is a good fit. Remember, it's okay to change your mind as you learn more about yourself and the world of work.

Case Studies on Exploring Passions and Interests

Real-Life Examples of Exploring Passions and Interests

There are countless examples of individuals who have successfully turned their passions and interests into careers or meaningful pursuits. Consider the story of a young entrepreneur who turned a passion for technology into a successful app development company. Or the artist who used social media to showcase their work and eventually opened their own gallery.

These real-life examples demonstrate how exploring and nurturing your passions can lead to opportunities that may not have been apparent at the outset. They show the importance of persistence, creativity, and the willingness to take risks.

Lessons Learned from Case Studies

From these case studies, we can learn several lessons. First, it's important to be proactive in pursuing your interests. Take the initiative to learn, create, and connect with others in your field of interest. Second, be adaptable. The path to turning your passions into a career may not be linear, and being open to change can lead to unexpected opportunities.

Lastly, believe in yourself and your vision. Confidence and a strong sense of self can help you navigate challenges and stay focused on your goals.

Activities for Exploring Passions and Interests

Practical Exercises for Exploring Passions and Interests

There are many practical exercises you can do to explore your passions and interests. Start by creating a vision board that represents your interests and aspirations. This can help you visualize your goals and stay motivated.

Another exercise is to conduct informational interviews with professionals in fields you're curious about. This can provide you with a realistic view of what it's like to work in those areas and help you build a network of contacts.

Reflective Activities for Exploring Passions and Interests

Reflective activities can also be valuable in exploring your passions and interests. Journaling about your experiences and feelings can help you process what you've learned and identify patterns in what you enjoy. Additionally, setting aside time for quiet reflection can allow you to listen to your inner voice and gain clarity on your passions.

Further Reading

Books to Boost Your Self-Discovery Journey

1. The 7 Habits of Highly Effective Teens by Sean Covey: This book provides a step-by-step guide to help teens improve self-image, build friendships, resist peer pressure, achieve their goals, and get along with their parents.
2. Quiet: The Power of Introverts in a World That Can't Stop Talking by Susan Cain: This book explores the valuable contributions of introverts and how they can harness their unique strengths.
3. Start Where You Are: A Journal for Self-Exploration by Meera Lee Patel: This interactive journal encourages self-reflection through writing, drawing, chart-making, and more.

Passions, Interests and Self-Confidence

How Exploring Passions and Interests Builds Self-Confidence

Exploring your passions and interests can significantly boost your self-confidence. As you engage in activities you love and develop skills in those areas, you'll gain a sense of competence and achievement. This can reinforce your belief in your abilities and increase your confidence to take on new challenges.

The Interplay Between Self-Confidence and Passions, Interests

There is a positive feedback loop between self-confidence

and exploring passions and interests. As you become more confident, you're more likely to pursue your interests with vigor, which in turn can lead to further skill development and even greater confidence. This cycle can propel you towards personal mastery and success in various areas of your life.

Passions, Interests and Goal Achievement

The Role of Passions and Interests in Achieving Goals

Passions and interests play a vital role in achieving goals. They provide motivation and a sense of purpose, making it easier to set and work towards goals that are meaningful to you. When you're passionate about something, you're more likely to put in the effort and persist through obstacles to reach your objectives.

Exploring Passions and Interests for Goal Achievement

To use your passions and interests for goal achievement, start by setting goals that are directly related to your passions. Create a plan that includes specific, measurable, achievable, relevant, and time-bound (SMART) goals. This structured approach can help you make consistent progress and maintain focus on what's important to you.

> Winfrey, a media mogul and philanthropist, believes that passion fuels energy. When you're passionate about something, you're more likely to put in the time and effort needed to succeed.
>
> "Don't aim for success if you want it; just do what you love and believe in, and it will come naturally." - David Frost
>
> Frost, a renowned television host and journalist, suggests that success is a byproduct of doing what you love. When you're passionate about what you do, success will follow.

The Power of Exploring

Passions and Interests

Reflecting on the Journey of Exploring Passions and Interests

Reflecting on the journey of exploring your passions and interests can be incredibly rewarding. It allows you to see how far you've come and how your interests have shaped your life. This reflection can also provide insights into future paths you may want to pursue and how you can continue to integrate your passions into your life.

Looking Forward: Passions and Interests in the Journey to Mastery

Looking forward, your passions and interests will continue to be a guiding force in your journey to personal mastery. They will help you make decisions that align with your values, overcome challenges, and achieve your full potential. Embrace your passions and interests, as they are key to living a life that is not only successful but also deeply fulfilling.

1. What is the role of passions and interests in personal mastery?

    A. They distract from the process of personal mastery
    B. They are essential as they provide motivation and direction
    C. They have no role in personal mastery
    D. They hinder personal mastery by causing confusion

2. What is one benefit of exploring passions and interests?

    A. It helps to improve your cooking skills
    B. It contributes to personal growth
    C. It helps to improve your math

skills

   D. It contributes to weight loss

3. What is a strategy for overcoming challenges in exploring passions and interests?

   A. Seeking support
   B. Ignoring the challenges
   C. Avoiding the challenges

   D. Giving up

13. MINDFULNESS AND SELF-AWARENESS

Understanding Mindfulness

What is Mindfulness?

Mindfulness is the practice of being fully present and engaged in the moment, aware of your thoughts and feelings without distraction or judgment. It involves a conscious direction of our awareness. We sometimes think of it as the state of being alert and open to life as it unfolds. Mindfulness is not about getting rid of thoughts, but rather recognizing and steering them with intention. It's about noticing when our minds have wandered and gently bringing our attention back to the present.

This practice originates from ancient Eastern traditions and has been integrated into Western psychology due to its benefits for mental health and well-being. Mindfulness can be cultivated through meditation, but it is not limited to it. It can be applied to any activity, such as eating, walking, or listening to someone speak. The key is to maintain a moment-by moment awareness of our thoughts, feelings, bodily sensations, and the surrounding environment with openness and curiosity.

The Role of Mindfulness in Personal Mastery

Mindfulness plays a significant role in personal mastery, which is the ongoing process of developing oneself to achieve one's highest potential. By fostering mindfulness, individuals can gain better control over their responses to life's challenges. It allows for a greater understanding of one's emotions and thoughts, which is crucial in making wise decisions and responding rather than reacting to situations.

In the context of personal mastery, mindfulness is a tool that helps to clear the mental clutter, providing a clearer vision of one's goals and the steps needed to achieve them. It enhances focus and concentration, which are essential for learning new skills and improving existing ones. Mindfulness also contributes to self-regulation, a key aspect of emotional intelligence, by helping individuals manage their emotions effectively.

The Importance of Mindfulness

Benefits of Mindfulness

The benefits of mindfulness are extensive and well-documented. Regular practice can lead to reductions in stress and anxiety, as it helps individuals to break free from the cycle of negative thinking. Mindfulness has been shown to improve mental clarity, concentration, and cognitive flexibility, which are all vital for learning and personal development.

Physically, mindfulness can lower blood pressure, reduce chronic pain, and improve sleep. It has also been linked to better immune system functioning. On an emotional level, mindfulness can lead to an increased capacity for empathy and compassion, both towards oneself and others. This can enhance relationships and social interactions, which are integral parts of a fulfilling life.

Mindfulness and Personal Growth

Mindfulness is a cornerstone of personal growth. It encourages a nonjudgmental acceptance of our present experience, which can lead to a more profound understanding of ourselves. This self-knowledge is the foundation upon which personal growth is built. By becoming more aware of our habitual reactions, we can start to make deliberate choices that align with our values and goals.

Furthermore, mindfulness can foster a growth mindset. With a focus on the present, individuals are more likely to embrace challenges, persist in the face of setbacks, and see effort as a path to mastery. This mindset is essential for personal growth, as it moves us away from a fixed perspective and towards a more flexible and dynamic understanding of our capabilities.

Practicing Mindfulness

Identifying Characteristics of Mindfulness

Mindfulness is characterized by several key attributes. The first is intention, which is the decision to cultivate awareness of the present moment. The second is attention, which is the practice of bringing focus to our experiences without getting caught up in them. The third is attitude, which involves approaching each moment with curiosity, openness, and acceptance, rather than with preconceived judgments or expectations.

These characteristics work together to create a mindful state. When we are mindful, we are actively engaged in the present, aware of our thoughts and actions, and accepting of our current state without trying to change it. This can be a challenging state to achieve, as it requires us to step back from our automatic thoughts and reactions, but with practice, it becomes more accessible.

Steps to Practicing Mindfulness

Practicing mindfulness can be done through a variety of methods, but the core steps remain consistent. The first step is to find a quiet space where you can relax without interruptions. Next, choose a point of focus, such as your breath, a word or phrase (mantra), or a visual object. Then, bring your attention to this focal point, fully engaging with it in the present moment.

As you focus, your mind will inevitably wander. This is normal and to be expected. The practice of mindfulness is not to prevent this from happening but to notice when it does and gently redirect your attention back to your chosen point of focus. This cycle of wandering and returning is the essence of mindfulness practice.

Maintaining Mindfulness Over Time

Maintaining mindfulness over time requires consistent practice. It can be helpful to incorporate mindfulness into your daily routine, setting aside specific times for formal practice, such as meditation, as well as practicing informally by bringing mindful awareness to everyday activities. The goal is to make mindfulness a habit, something that becomes an integral part of your life.

It's also important to be patient and kind to yourself as you practice. Mindfulness is a skill that takes time to develop, and there will be days when it feels more challenging than others. Recognizing and accepting this as part of the process is itself an act of mindfulness.

Understanding Self-Awareness

What is Self-Awareness?

Self-awareness is the conscious knowledge of one's own character, feelings, motives, and desires. It involves understanding your own needs, desires, failings, habits, and everything else that makes you tick. The more you know about yourself, the better you are at adapting life changes that suit your needs.

Unlike mindfulness, which focuses on the present moment, self-awareness extends to understanding past behaviors and predicting future ones. It's a deep understanding of your emotional and psychological makeup, which can lead to profound insights into why you react the way you do and how you can improve your behavior.

The Role of Self-Awareness in Personal Mastery

Self-awareness is a vital component of personal mastery because it is the mechanism through which personal change can occur. Without self-awareness, we cannot understand what needs to be improved or developed. It allows us to see where our thoughts and emotions are guiding us and gives us the power to take control of our actions.

With self-awareness, we can objectively evaluate our strengths and weaknesses, set realistic goals, and monitor our progress. It also helps us to understand how our behavior affects others, which is crucial for building and maintaining healthy relationships. In essence, self-awareness is the foundation upon which personal growth and mastery are built.

Boosts Emotional Intelligence: Self-awareness is the first step in developing emotional intelligence. It allows you to understand your emotions, which can help you manage them effectively.

Enhances Leadership Skills: Leaders who are self-aware can understand their strengths and weaknesses, which can help them lead more effectively.

Increases Empathy: When you are self-aware, you can understand your own emotions, which can help you empathize with others and understand their emotions better.

Reduces Stress: Self-awareness can help you understand what causes you stress and how you react to it, which can help you manage stress more effectively.

So, developing self-awareness can not only help you achieve personal mastery but also improve your overall quality of life!

The Importance of Self-Awareness

Benefits of Self-Awareness

The benefits of self-awareness are manifold. It leads to better decision-making because you are more clear on your values and goals. It also enhances your ability to communicate with others, as you understand your emotions and can express them more clearly. Self-awareness is associated with higher job satisfaction and performance because it aligns your work with your personal values and capabilities.

On a personal level, self-awareness can lead to increased happiness and life satisfaction. It allows you to live a more authentic life, as you are guided by your true desires and values, rather than being swayed by external pressures. It also helps in managing stress and navigating complex social situations by providing a clearer understanding of your emotional responses.

Self-Awareness and Personal Growth

Self-awareness is a catalyst for personal growth. It enables you to identify the areas of your life that need attention or change. With this knowledge, you can develop strategies to overcome obstacles and enhance your strengths. Self-awareness also promotes a deeper understanding of your learning processes, which can accelerate your growth and development.

As you become more self-aware, you may also become more accepting of your faults, which can lead to greater self-compassion and a reduction in self-criticism. This acceptance is not about resignation but about recognizing your humanity and using that knowledge to foster growth.

Biographical Snapshot

Jon Kabat-Zinn: A Pioneer in Mindfulness

Jon Kabat-Zinn is a renowned scientist, writer, and meditation teacher who is widely recognized for his work in bringing mindfulness into the mainstream of medicine and society. His teachings have had a profound impact on the field of self-awareness and personal growth.

Early Life and Education

Born on June 5, 1944, in New York City, Kabat-Zinn earned a Ph.D. in molecular biology from the Massachusetts Institute of Technology in 1971. His interest in mindfulness began in his early twenties when he attended a lecture about meditation.

Contributions to Mindfulness

In 1979, Kabat-Zinn founded the Stress Reduction Clinic at the
University of Massachusetts Medical School, where he adapted

Buddhist teachings on mindfulness and developed the Mindfulness Based Stress Reduction (MBSR) program. This program has been widely accepted in the west and has been proven to help people cope with stress, pain, and illness.

Impact on Self-Awareness

Kabat-Zinn's work has greatly contributed to the understanding of self-awareness. His teachings emphasize the importance of being present and fully engaged with our current experiences, which is a key aspect of self-awareness.

His work has helped countless individuals to cultivate a deeper sense of self-understanding and personal growth.

Building Self-Awareness

Identifying Characteristics of Self-Awareness

Self-awareness is characterized by an honest self-reflection, an understanding of personal values, and an awareness of how one's actions affect both oneself and others. It also involves recognizing patterns in one's thoughts and behaviors, as well as the ability to predict one's reactions to certain situations.

Another characteristic of self-awareness is the willingness to learn and grow. This includes seeking feedback from others and using it constructively to make positive changes. It also means being open to new experiences and ideas that can lead to greater self-understanding.

Steps to Building Self-Awareness

Building self-awareness is a process that can be developed through several steps. The first step is to engage in regular self-reflection, which can be done through journaling, meditation, or simply taking time to think about your day and your reactions to events. The second step is to ask for and be open to feedback from others, as they can provide an outside perspective on your behavior.

Another important step is to set personal goals that align with your values and to monitor your progress towards these goals. This can help you understand what motivates you and how you can continue to grow. Finally, practicing mindfulness can also enhance self-awareness, as it brings your attention to your thoughts and feelings in the present moment.

Maintaining Self-Awareness Over Time

Maintaining self-awareness over time requires a commitment to continuous self-exploration and self-improvement. It involves regularly revisiting your goals and values to ensure they still align with your true self. It also means continuing to seek feedback and using it to refine your understanding of yourself.

Another key to maintaining self-awareness is to stay curious about yourself and why you do the things you do. This curiosity can lead to a lifelong journey of discovery and growth. It's also important to practice self-compassion, as this can help you accept yourself as you are while still striving to improve.

Overcoming Challenges in Mindfulness and Self-Awareness

Identifying Challenges

One of the main challenges in practicing mindfulness and self-awareness is dealing with the discomfort that can come from facing our true thoughts and emotions. It can be difficult to sit with negative feelings or to recognize aspects of ourselves that we may not like. Distractions and a busy lifestyle can also make it challenging to find time for self-reflection and mindfulness practices.

Another challenge is the tendency to be overly critical of oneself, which can hinder the process of self-awareness. It's common to become frustrated with the slow pace of change or to feel discouraged when old habits resurface. These challenges can be obstacles to maintaining a consistent practice of mindfulness and self-awareness. Be gentle with yourself. As mentioned earlier, the voice in our head can be the most critical. Think about what you would say to a friend. How would your voice sound? What are the gentle and encouraging words you would use with them. Now try that on yourself. Feels odd, right? Keep trying. It gets easier. You're doing great.

Strategies for Overcoming Challenges

To overcome these challenges, it's important to set realistic expectations and to approach mindfulness and self-awareness with patience and kindness. It can be helpful to start with small, manageable practices and gradually build up to longer periods of reflection or meditation.

Developing a regular routine can also make it easier to incorporate mindfulness and self-awareness into your daily life. Finding a community or a support group can provide encouragement and accountability. Additionally, learning to recognize and counteract self-critical thoughts with self-compassion can help you maintain your practice even when it feels difficult.

Seeking Support for Challenges

If you find it particularly challenging to maintain mindfulness and self-awareness practices, seeking support can be beneficial. This support can come from friends, family, or mental health professionals who can provide guidance and encouragement. There are also many resources available, such as books, online courses, and workshops, that can offer strategies and support for deepening your practice.

Joining mindfulness or meditation groups can also provide a sense of community and shared experience that can be motivating. Remember that seeking support is a sign of strength and an important step in your journey towards personal mastery.

Case Studies on Mindfulness and Self-awareness

Real-Life Examples of Mindfulness and Self-Awareness

There are many inspiring real-life examples of individuals who have used mindfulness and self-awareness to transform their lives. One such example is a person who overcame severe anxiety by incorporating daily mindfulness meditation into their routine. Through this practice, they learned to observe their anxious thoughts without judgment and to bring their focus back to the present moment, reducing the power of those thoughts over time.

Another example is a business leader who used self-awareness to improve their leadership skills. By seeking feedback from their team and reflecting on their own behavior, they were able to identify areas for improvement and make changes that led to a more positive and productive work environment.

Lessons Learned from Case Studies

These case studies highlight the transformative power of mindfulness and self-awareness. They show that with dedication and practice, it is possible to change deeply ingrained patterns of thinking and behavior. They also demonstrate the importance of self-compassion and patience in the process of personal growth.

Another lesson is the value of feedback and the role it plays in developing self-awareness. By being open to the perspectives of others, we can gain insights that are not always visible from our own viewpoint. These case studies serve as motivation and evidence that mindfulness and self-awareness are powerful tools for personal mastery.

Activities for Building Mindfulness and Self-awareness

Practical Exercises for Building Mindfulness and Self-Awareness

There are many practical exercises that can help build mindfulness and self-awareness. One simple exercise is the "Five Senses" practice, where you take a moment to focus on one thing you can see, hear, touch, taste, and smell. This practice can quickly bring you into the present moment and heighten your awareness of your surroundings.

Another exercise is the "Body Scan" meditation, where you focus on each part of your body in turn, observing any sensations without judgment. This can help you become more attuned to your physical presence and can be particularly helpful in managing stress and anxiety.

A tool that helped me when I first learned how to meditate is to focus on an object in your mind. At first, I would think about my grandfather's face. But he had recently passed away and seeing him just made me sad. So, I thought about his last name, which was LaRosa. Meaning – "the rose" in Italian. So, I would start by thinking about a rose in my mind's eye. I would look at the rose pedals, the stem, the thorns. It helped me. As I got better at meditation I would imagine the rose spinning. The more clarify of focus the faster the rose will spin in my mind's eye.

Now you try.

Think of an object.

Try to make it spin in your mind's eye.

See if you can do it and hold clarity of focus.

Congratulations – you're meditating!

Reflective Activities for Building Mindfulness and Self-Awareness

Reflective activities, such as journaling, can also be beneficial for building mindfulness and self-awareness. Writing about your experiences and emotions can help you process them more deeply and gain insights into your patterns of thought and behavior. Reflecting on your day before bed, perhaps by noting three things you were grateful for, can also promote a positive mindset and greater self-awareness.

Engaging in regular conversations with a trusted friend or mentor about your personal growth can also be a reflective activity that enhances self-awareness. These conversations can provide valuable feedback and different perspectives on your journey.

Mindfulness, Self-Awareness and Self-confidence

How Mindfulness and Self-Awareness Builds Self-Confidence

Mindfulness and self-awareness contribute to self-confidence by helping you understand and accept yourself as you are. This acceptance can lead to a stronger sense of self-worth and a belief in your ability to handle life's challenges. As you become more aware of your strengths and how to leverage them, your confidence in your abilities grows.

Additionally, as you become more mindful, you learn to trust your judgment and to make decisions based on your true values and goals. This can lead to a greater sense of agency and empowerment, which are key components of self-confidence.

The Interplay Between Self-Confidence, Mindfulness and Self-Awareness

The relationship between self-confidence, mindfulness, and self-awareness is dynamic and reinforcing. As you become more self-aware, you gain a clearer understanding of your capabilities, which boosts your confidence. This increased confidence can then encourage you to engage more deeply with mindfulness practices, leading to even greater self-awareness and confidence.

Mindfulness can also help reduce self-doubt by bringing your attention back to the present and away from worries about the past or future. This present-moment focus can help you build a stable foundation of self-confidence that is not easily shaken

1. What is mindfulness?

A. The ability to multitask effectively
B. The practice of being present and fully engaged with whatever we're doing at the moment
C. The ability to predict future events
D. The ability to remember past events clearly

2. Which of the following is NOT a benefit of mindfulness?

    A. Reduced stress
    B. Increased multitasking ability
    C. Enhanced emotional intelligence

    D. Improved focus and concentration

3. What is self-awareness?

    A. The ability to understand others' emotions
    B. The ability to understand and be aware of one's own emotions, thoughts, and behaviors
    C. The ability to predict future events

    D. The ability to remember past events clearly

4. Which of the following is NOT a step in building self-awareness?

    A Seeking feedback from others
    B. Ignoring your feelings
    C. Practicing mindfulness

    D. Keeping a journal

5. How do mindfulness and self-awareness contribute to self-confidence?

    A. By helping you predict future events
    B. By helping you multitask effectively
    C. By helping you understand your strengths and

weaknesses
D. By helping you remember past events clearly

14. FINDING BALANCE IN LIFE

Understanding Life Balance

What is Life Balance?

Life balance is a concept that refers to the equilibrium between the various aspects of a person's life. This balance is not about allocating an equal amount of time to each area, but rather about finding a harmonious distribution of energy and focus that aligns with one's values and priorities. Life balance encompasses the management of personal, social, academic, and extracurricular activities. It is the delicate act of juggling these areas to achieve a sense of fulfillment and well-being.

Achieving life balance is a personal journey, as everyone has different goals, responsibilities, and definitions of success. For some, balance might mean spending more time with family, while for others, it could involve dedicating time to personal development or hobbies. The key is to understand that life balance is fluid and can change over time as one's circumstances and priorities evolve.

The Role of Life Balance in Personal Mastery

Personal mastery is the ongoing process of self-improvement and self-understanding. Life balance plays a crucial role in this journey, as it allows individuals to cultivate a lifestyle that supports their growth and aspirations. When life is balanced, people are better equipped to focus on their goals, manage stress, and maintain a positive outlook.

A balanced life provides the foundation for personal mastery by ensuring that no single aspect of life overshadows the others. This equilibrium helps prevent burnout and promotes sustained engagement with one's passions and responsibilities. By prioritizing life balance, individuals can nurture their talents, build resilience, and enhance their ability to adapt to change.

The Importance of Life Balance

Benefits of Life Balance

Life balance offers numerous benefits that contribute to an individual's overall well-being. These benefits include improved mental and physical health, increased productivity, and stronger relationships. When life is balanced, stress levels are typically lower, leading to a more positive mood and a clearer mind. This state of well-being allows individuals to be more present and engaged in their daily activities.

Additionally, life balance can lead to better time management, as individuals learn to prioritize tasks and allocate their time more effectively. This skill is particularly important for teenagers, who are often balancing schoolwork, extracurricular activities, and social lives. By understanding the importance of balance, they can make informed decisions about how to spend their time, leading to a more fulfilling and less stressful life.

Life Balance and Personal Growth

Personal growth is an integral part of adolescence, a time when individuals are discovering their identities and potential. Life balance supports this process by providing the space and time needed for self-exploration and development. When teenagers have a balanced life, they are more likely to engage in a variety of experiences that contribute to their growth, such as trying new activities, developing new skills, and forming meaningful relationships.

Furthermore, life balance encourages reflection and introspection, allowing individuals to assess their progress and set new goals. This reflective practice is essential for personal growth, as it helps teenagers understand their strengths and areas for improvement. By maintaining balance, they can continue to evolve and reach new heights in their journey to personal mastery.

Test Your Knowledge:

How well do you understand the concept of life balance and its impact on personal growth? Let's find out! Answer the following questions:

1. What is the role of life balance in personal growth during adolescence?

2. How does life balance contribute to trying new activities, developing new skills, and forming meaningful relationships?

3. Why is reflection and introspection important in maintaining life balance?

4. How does understanding your strengths and areas for improvement contribute to personal growth?

Reflect on these questions and write down your answers. Discuss them with your peers or your teacher to deepen your understanding of life balance and personal growth.

Achieving Life Balance

Identifying Characteristics of a Balanced Life

A balanced life is characterized by a sense of control over one's time and choices. It involves having clear priorities and aligning one's actions with those priorities. Characteristics of a balanced life include a healthy work life balance, time for self-care, and the ability to pursue personal interests and hobbies. It also involves having strong, supportive relationships and engaging in activities that bring joy and satisfaction.

Another characteristic of a balanced life is flexibility. Life is unpredictable, and the ability to adapt to changing circumstances is crucial for maintaining balance. This means being willing to reassess and adjust one's schedule and priorities as needed. A balanced life is not static; it is dynamic and responsive to the individual's evolving needs and goals.

Steps to Achieving Life Balance

Achieving life balance requires intentional effort and planning. The first step is to identify one's values and priorities. This involves reflecting on what is most important and what brings the most fulfillment. Once these priorities are established, individuals can set goals and create a plan to integrate these priorities into their daily lives.

The next step is to assess one's current commitments and responsibilities. This assessment allows individuals to determine where their time is being spent and to identify any areas that may be out of balance. From there, they can adjust, such as delegating tasks, setting boundaries, or eliminating unnecessary activities.

Time management is also a critical component of achieving life balance. This includes creating a schedule that allocates time for work, rest, and play. It's important to be realistic about what can be accomplished in a day and to build in time for breaks and relaxation. Additionally, learning to say "no" to requests that do not align with one's priorities is an essential skill for maintaining balance.

Maintaining Life Balance Over Time

Maintaining life balance over time requires ongoing attention and adjustment. It's important to regularly check in with oneself to ensure that the balance is still in line with one's priorities. This may involve revisiting goals, reassessing commitments, and making changes to one's schedule as needed.

It's also essential to be proactive in managing stress and avoiding burnout. This can be achieved through self-care practices such as exercise, meditation, and spending time with loved ones. Additionally, seeking feedback from trusted friends or mentors can provide valuable insights into how to maintain balance and continue growing personally and professionally.

Overcoming Challenges in Achieving Life Balance

Identifying Challenges

Challenges to achieving life balance can come in many forms, including overcommitment, lack of time management skills, and external pressures from peers or society. It's important to recognize these challenges early on to address them effectively. For teenagers, common challenges might include managing academic demands, navigating social dynamics, and coping with the expectations of parents and teachers.

Another challenge is the influence of technology and social media, which can lead to constant connectivity and difficulty disconnecting from the digital world. This can create a sense of being always "on" and can interfere with one's ability to relax and recharge. Identifying these challenges is the first step toward finding balance.

Strategies for Overcoming Challenges

Overcoming challenges to life balance involves developing strategies that work for the individual. One effective strategy is to set clear boundaries around work and personal time. This might mean designating certain hours of the day for schoolwork and others for relaxation or hobbies. It's also helpful to prioritize tasks based on urgency and importance, focusing on what needs to be done now and what can wait.

Learning to delegate tasks and ask for help when needed can also alleviate the pressure to do everything oneself. Additionally, practicing mindfulness and being present in the moment can help individuals avoid becoming overwhelmed by future tasks or commitments. Finally, taking regular breaks and ensuring adequate rest are crucial for maintaining energy and focus.

Seeking Support for Challenges

Seeking support from others is a valuable tool in overcoming challenges to life balance. This support can come from family, friends, teachers, or counselors who can offer guidance, encouragement, and practical assistance. Joining a support group or club with like-minded individuals can also provide a sense of community and shared experiences.

Professional help, such as coaching or therapy, can be beneficial for those who need more structured support. These professionals can help individuals develop personalized strategies for achieving balance and provide accountability along the way. It's important to remember that seeking support is a sign of strength, not weakness, and is an essential part of the journey to personal mastery.

The Role of Life Balance in Stress Management

Understanding Stress Management

Stress management is the process of identifying and handling stress in a healthy way. It involves recognizing the sources of stress, understanding how they affect one's life, and implementing strategies to manage or reduce their impact. Effective stress management is crucial for maintaining mental and physical health, as well as for achieving life balance.

Stress can arise from various areas of life, including academic pressures, social relationships, and personal expectations. By managing stress effectively, individuals can prevent it from becoming overwhelming and disrupting their balance. This involves both proactive strategies, such as regular exercise and relaxation techniques, and reactive strategies, such as seeking support when stress levels become too high.

Life Balance and Stress Management

Life balance is inherently connected to stress management. When life is balanced, stress is more manageable because there is a sense of control and order. A balanced life allows for time to address stressors head-on, rather than letting them accumulate. It also provides opportunities for rest and recovery, which are essential for resilience in the face of stress.

Conversely, when life is out of balance, stress can quickly escalate. This can lead to a cycle of increased stress and decreased balance, making it difficult to break free. By prioritizing life balance, individuals can create a buffer against stress and maintain a healthier, more manageable lifestyle.

Achieving Stress Management through Life Balance

Achieving stress management through life balance involves integrating stress-reducing activities into one's daily routine. This might include physical activities like yoga or running, creative outlets such as art or music, or relaxation practices like meditation or deep breathing exercises. It's also important to build in time for social connections, as relationships can be a source of support and comfort during stressful times.

Time management is another key aspect of stress management. By organizing one's time effectively, individuals can reduce the feeling of being rushed or overwhelmed. This includes setting realistic goals, breaking tasks into manageable steps, and allowing for flexibility in one's schedule. By managing time wisely, individuals can reduce stress and maintain a sense of balance in their lives.

Case Studies on Life Balance

Real-Life Examples of Achieving Life Balance

There are many inspiring examples of individuals who have successfully achieved life balance. These case studies often involve people who have faced significant challenges but have found ways to integrate their work, personal interests, and relationships into a cohesive and fulfilling life. For instance, a student athlete who manages to excel in sports while maintaining high academic standards and a social life can serve as a powerful example of life balance.

Another example might be a teenager who has started a small business or community project. Despite the demands of entrepreneurship, they find time for self-care, family, and friends. These real-life examples provide valuable insights into the strategies and mindsets that contribute to a balanced life.

Lessons Learned from Case Studies

Case studies on life balance reveal several common lessons. One key takeaway is the importance of setting clear priorities and sticking to them. Successful individuals often have a strong sense of what is most important to them and make decisions that align with these values. Another lesson is the value of flexibility and the willingness to adapt to changing circumstances. Life is dynamic, and the ability to pivot and adjust one's approach to balance is crucial.

Additionally, these case studies highlight the role of support systems in achieving balance. Whether it's family, friends, or mentors, having people to turn to for advice and encouragement can make a significant difference. Finally, the case studies demonstrate that achieving life balance is an ongoing process that requires continuous effort and self-reflection.

Activities for Achieving Life Balance

Practical Exercises for Achieving Life Balance

There are several practical exercises that can help individuals work towards achieving life balance. Time audits, where one tracks their activities for a week, can provide insight into how time is being spent and where adjustments might be needed. Goal-setting workshops can help clarify priorities and create actionable plans for integrating those priorities into daily life.

Mindfulness practices, such as meditation or journaling, can also be beneficial. These activities encourage individuals to be present and aware of their thoughts and feelings, which can lead to better decision-making and a more balanced life. Additionally, engaging in role-playing scenarios can help teenagers practice setting boundaries and managing commitments, which are essential skills for maintaining balance.

Reflective Activities for Achieving Life Balance

Reflective activities are another important aspect of achieving life balance. These activities encourage individuals to think deeply about their lives and the choices they make. Examples include writing reflective essays on personal values, creating vision boards that represent one's goals and aspirations, and participating in guided discussions about balance and well-being.

When I was eighteen and away at Loyola University, I found that sitting in a secluded area alone to think and journal was my key to unlock the shackles of anxiety. If I didn't have a loved one around to speak to – I would write in my journal what I would say to them if they were in the room with me. It's how I started to learn how to write and even write poetry. Plus, it helped me from feeling homesick.

Gratitude exercises, such as keeping a gratitude journal, can also promote balance by focusing on the positive aspects of life. Reflecting on accomplishments and challenges can provide perspective and motivate individuals to continue striving for a balanced and fulfilling life.

Life Balance and Self-Confidence

How Life Balance Builds Self-Confidence

Life balance can have a profound impact on self-confidence. When individuals feel in control of their lives and can manage their responsibilities effectively, they often experience a boost in self-esteem. This sense of accomplishment reinforces the belief in one's abilities and can lead to greater confidence in tackling new challenges.

Additionally, a balanced life allows for personal growth and the development of new skills. As teenagers explore different interests and activities, they build a more diverse set of abilities, which can enhance their self-confidence. The support and positive feedback from others that often come with a balanced life also contribute to a stronger sense of self-worth.

The Interplay Between Self-Confidence and Life Balance

The relationship between self-confidence and life balance is reciprocal. Not only does life balance contribute to self-confidence, but self-confidence can also facilitate the achievement of life balance. Confident individuals are more likely to set boundaries, prioritize their well-being, and make choices that align with their values. This assertiveness helps them maintain balance in the face of external pressures and challenges.

Furthermore, self-confidence enables individuals to trust their judgment and make decisions that support their goals for balance. It also encourages them to seek out new experiences and opportunities for growth, which can further enhance their life balance and overall satisfaction.

Life Balance and Goal Achievement

The Role of Life Balance in Achieving Goals

Life balance is essential for goal achievement. When individuals have a balanced approach to life, they are better able to focus on their objectives and take consistent action towards them. Balance ensures that there is time and energy dedicated to pursuing goals without neglecting other important areas of life.

By maintaining balance, individuals can avoid burnout and sustain their motivation over the long term. This steady progress is often more effective than sporadic bursts of effort that can result from an unbalanced lifestyle. Additionally, a balanced life provides the mental clarity and emotional stability needed to overcome obstacles and persevere in the face of setbacks.

Achieving Life Balance for Goal Achievement

To use life balance as a tool for goal achievement, individuals must integrate their goals into their daily routines. This might involve setting aside specific times for goal-related activities, breaking goals down into smaller, manageable tasks, and regularly reviewing progress. It's also important to celebrate small victories along the way, as this reinforces the connection between balance and achievement.

Another aspect of achieving life balance for goal achievement is to ensure that goals are aligned with one's values and priorities. This alignment creates a sense of purpose and meaning, which can be powerful motivators. By pursuing goals that resonate with their core beliefs, individuals can maintain balance and increase their chances of success.

Famous Quotes

"The key is not to prioritize what's on your schedule, but to schedule your priorities." - Stephen Covey

This quote emphasizes the importance of aligning your goals with your values and priorities, as mentioned in the text. By scheduling your priorities, you are integrating your goals into your daily routines, which is a key aspect of achieving life balance for goal achievement.

"Success is not the key to happiness. Happiness is the key to success.
If you love what you are doing, you will be successful." - Albert
Schweitzer

Albert Schweitzer's quote reinforces the idea that pursuing goals that resonate with your core beliefs can increase your chances of success. It's not just about achieving success, but about finding happiness in the process.

"The greater danger for most of us lies not in setting our aim too high and falling short; but in setting our aim too low, and achieving our mark." - Michelangelo

Michelangelo's quote encourages us to set high goals for ourselves.

Even if we fall short, we are still achieving more than if we set our goals too low. This quote can inspire you to break your goals down into smaller, manageable tasks and regularly review your progress.

The Power of Life Balance

Reflecting on the Journey of Achieving Life Balance

Reflecting on the journey of achieving life balance is an important part of personal mastery. It allows individuals to appreciate the progress they have made and to learn from their experiences. Reflection can also provide insights into what strategies have been most effective and what areas may still need attention.

This reflective process is not only about looking back but also about planning for the future. By understanding the past, individuals can make informed decisions about how to maintain and improve their life balance moving forward. This ongoing reflection is a key component of a balanced life and personal growth.

Looking Forward: Life Balance in the Journey to Mastery

Looking forward, life balance will continue to play a vital role in the journey to personal mastery. As individuals grow and their circumstances change, their approach to balance will need to evolve as well. The skills and mindsets developed through the pursuit of life balance will serve as a foundation for future challenges and opportunities.

---

1. What is Life Balance?

    A. The ability to manage all aspects of life in a way that promotes well-being and personal satisfaction
    B. The ability to do everything perfectly

C. Never experiencing stress or challenges
D. Having equal amounts of work and leisure time

2. What is one benefit of achieving Life Balance?

    A. It can contribute to personal growth and well-being
    B. You will become perfect
    C. You will never face any challenges

    D. You will have more time for leisure activities

3. What is a strategy for achieving Life Balance?

    A. Ignoring personal needs and focusing only on work or school
    B. Doing everything at once to save time
    C. Identifying and prioritizing what is most important in your life

    D. Avoiding all forms of stress and challenges

4. How does Life Balance contribute to stress management?

    A. It ensures that you will never feel stressed
    B. It allows you to avoid all stressful situations
    C. It provides a framework for managing different aspects of life, reducing the likelihood of feeling overwhelmed
    D. It eliminates all sources of stress

5. How does Life Balance relate to self-confidence?

    A. Life Balance and self-confidence are unrelated concepts
    B. Achieving Life Balance can boost self-confidence by fostering a sense of personal mastery and control
    C. Life Balance has no impact on self-confidence

D. Life Balance reduces self-confidence because it requires admitting weaknesses

15. MAKING DECISIONS AND TAKING OWNERSHIP

Understanding Decision Making

What is Decision Making?

Decision making is the process of choosing between two or more courses of action. In the broader process of problem-solving, decision making involves choosing a specific solution from the available options. When making decisions, individuals must weigh the positives and negatives of each option, consider all the alternatives, and predict the possible outcomes. Decision making is a core skill that applies to various aspects of life.

A decision can be as simple as choosing what to eat for breakfast or as complex as deciding which college to attend. Each decision carries certain consequences – both intended and unintended. The ability to make informed, timely, and effective decisions is a key component of personal mastery. It involves critical thinking, the ability to anticipate outcomes, and the confidence to take action.

The Role of Decision Making in Personal Mastery

Personal mastery is about having a clear understanding of your personal vision, values, and goals. Decision making plays a pivotal role in personal mastery as it directly influences the direction of your life's journey. Every decision you make shapes your experiences, your character, and the opportunities that come your way.

Effective decision making requires self-awareness, as you need to understand your preferences, strengths, and weaknesses. It also involves self-regulation, as you must manage emotions to prevent them from clouding your judgment. By mastering the art of decision making, you empower yourself to take control of your life and steer it towards your desired outcomes.

The Importance of Decision Making

Benefits of Decision Making

Making decisions can lead to a multitude of benefits. It can improve your problem-solving skills, enhance your leadership abilities, and increase your autonomy. Decisions lead to actions, which lead to results. When you make decisions effectively, you're more likely to achieve your goals and fulfill your potential.

Additionally, decision making can lead to greater satisfaction in life. When you actively make choices that align with your values and goals, you feel a sense of accomplishment and purpose. This proactive approach to life can reduce feelings of helplessness and increase your sense of control over your destiny.

Decision Making and Personal Growth

Personal growth is often the result of stepping out of your comfort zone and making tough decisions. When faced with challenging situations, the decisions you make can lead to personal development and growth. Through the process of making decisions, you learn about prioritization, the consequences of your actions, and the importance of adaptability and flexibility.

Moreover, decision making is a skill that improves with practice. The more decisions you make, the better you become at analyzing situations, anticipating outcomes, and trusting your instincts. This growth is a fundamental aspect of personal mastery and contributes to your overall maturity and wisdom.

Effective Decision Making

Identifying Characteristics of Effective Decision Making

Effective decision making is characterized by several key attributes. First, it involves gathering relevant information and considering a wide range of potential solutions. It also requires clear thinking and the ability to remain unbiased while evaluating the options.

Another characteristic of effective decision making is the consideration of both short-term and long-term consequences. Effective decision-makers also have the courage to make tough choices and the resilience to deal with the results of those decisions, whether they are positive or negative.

Steps to Effective Decision Making

The process of effective decision making can be broken down into several steps. The first step is to clearly define the problem or decision that needs to be made. Once the issue is clear, the next step is to gather information and identify possible solutions or courses of action.

After evaluating the options, the third step is to weigh the evidence and consider the pros and cons of each choice. This leads to the fourth step, which is making the decision. Finally, the last step is to review your decision and its consequences, learning from the experience and adjusting for future decisions.

Maintaining Effective Decision Making Over Time

To maintain effective decision making over time, it's important to reflect on past decisions and their outcomes.

This reflection can provide valuable insights into your decision-making process and help you improve it. It's also crucial to stay informed and continue learning, as this will provide you with the knowledge and tools needed to make better decisions in the future.

Additionally, maintaining a network of trusted advisors and seeking feedback can help you see different perspectives and avoid blind spots in your decision making. Staying open to new ideas and being willing to adapt your approach as necessary are also key to maintaining effective decision-making skills over time.

Understanding Ownership

What is Ownership?

Ownership is the act of taking responsibility for your choices and their outcomes, including the actions you take and their impact on your life and others. It means acknowledging that you are the primary agent of change in your life and accepting the consequences of your actions, whether good or bad.

Ownership goes beyond just making decisions; it involves a commitment to follow through with actions and see them to completion. It's about taking control of your life's narrative and being accountable for the path you choose to follow.

The Role of Ownership in Personal Mastery

Ownership is a fundamental aspect of personal mastery. It empowers individuals to take control of their lives and to shape their destinies. When you take ownership, you move from being a passive observer to an active participant in your life's journey.

Taking ownership means being proactive about your personal

development, setting goals, and working towards them with determination. It also means being honest with yourself about your strengths and weaknesses and taking steps to improve where necessary. Ownership is about embracing the power you have to make changes and to grow as an individual.

The Importance of Taking Ownership

Benefits of Taking Ownership

Taking ownership has numerous benefits. It fosters a sense of independence and self-efficacy, as you recognize that you have the power to influence your life's direction. Ownership also leads to increased motivation and engagement, as you are more invested in the outcomes of your actions.

Furthermore, taking ownership can improve your performance, both personally and professionally, as it encourages a sense of pride in your work and a desire to achieve high standards. It also builds integrity and earns you respect from others, as it demonstrates accountability and responsibility.

Ownership and Personal Growth

Personal growth is closely tied to taking ownership. When you take responsibility for your actions and decisions, you are more likely to reflect on your experiences and learn from them. This reflection can lead to personal insights and a deeper understanding of yourself, which are essential for personal growth.

Taking ownership also means embracing the lessons that come from both successes and failures. It involves a willingness to take risks and step out of your comfort zone, which are critical for growth and development. By taking ownership, you set the stage for continuous improvement and lifelong learning.

Think & Reflect

Reflect on a time when you took ownership of a situation. What was the situation? What actions did you take? How did it make you feel?
What did you learn from the experience?

Consider a time when you avoided taking ownership. Why did you avoid it? What was the outcome? How might the situation have been

Taking Ownership Effectively

Identifying Characteristics of Effective Ownership

Effective ownership is characterized by a proactive approach to life. It involves setting clear goals, planning to achieve them, and taking consistent action towards those goals. It also means being accountable for your actions and their outcomes, and not shifting blame onto others or external circumstances.

Another characteristic of effective ownership is the ability to reflect on and learn from both successes and failures. It involves a commitment to personal growth and the courage to make necessary changes. Effective ownership also includes the ability to communicate openly and honestly with others, especially when it comes to expectations and responsibilities.

Steps to Taking Ownership Effectively

The first step to taking ownership effectively is to set clear and achievable goals. Once you have a goal in mind, the next step is to create a plan of action and commit to following through with it. This involves breaking down the goal into smaller, manageable tasks and setting deadlines for each task.

The third step is to monitor your progress and adjust as needed. This might involve seeking feedback, learning new skills, or changing your approach. The final step is to take responsibility for the outcomes of your actions, whether they meet your expectations or not, and to use those outcomes as learning experiences for future endeavors.

Maintaining Ownership Over Time

Maintaining ownership over time requires a commitment to continuous self-improvement and learning. It involves regularly evaluating your goals and the steps you're taking to achieve them and being willing to make changes when necessary.

It's also important to stay resilient in the face of setbacks and to view them as opportunities for growth. Building a support network can help you maintain ownership, as it provides encouragement and advice when you need it. Finally, maintaining ownership means consistently practicing self-reflection and being honest with yourself about your strengths and weaknesses.

Overcoming Challenges in Decision Making and Taking Ownership

Identifying Challenges

One of the main challenges in decision making and taking ownership is dealing with uncertainty. It can be difficult to make decisions when the outcomes are unknown or when there is a risk of failure. Another challenge is overcoming fear, as fear of making the wrong decision can lead to indecision or procrastination.

Taking ownership can also be challenging when faced with external pressures or when you're unsure of your abilities. It can be tempting to shift blame or make excuses rather than taking responsibility for your actions.

Strategies for Overcoming Challenges

To overcome these challenges, it's important to develop a strong sense of self-confidence and to trust in your ability to make good decisions. This can be achieved through practice and by starting with smaller decisions before tackling larger ones.

When it comes to taking ownership, it's helpful to focus on

what you can control and to let go of what you can't. It's also important to develop a growth mindset and to view challenges as opportunities to learn and improve. Seeking support from others can also provide the encouragement and perspective needed to overcome these challenges.

Seeking Support for Challenges

Seeking support is a key strategy for overcoming challenges in decision making and taking ownership. This support can come from mentors, coaches, friends, or family members. These individuals can offer advice, share their own experiences, and provide a different perspective on the situation. I always tell my girls – I'm not smart, I've just been around longer than you. Find someone who has been exposed the scenario you're trying to master and see if they're experience can help you. It's just advice, you can ignore it if you wish. Choosing to seek guidance can be the smartest decision you make.

> Intuition: Sometimes, your gut feeling can guide you to make the right decision. This is called intuition. It's based on your past experiences and knowledge.
>
> Pros and Cons: One common method of decision making is to list the pros and cons of each option. This can help you weigh the potential benefits and drawbacks of each choice.
>
> Consultation: Seeking advice from others can provide you with different perspectives and insights that you might not have considered on your own.

Similarly, taking ownership is a crucial part of personal growth. It means accepting responsibility for your actions and their outcomes, whether they're good or bad. It's about being accountable for your decisions and learning from

POTENTIAL

your mistakes.

Remember, it's okay to ask for help when you're struggling. Seeking support is not a sign of weakness, but a sign of strength and wisdom.

Case Studies on Decision Making and Taking Ownership

Real-Life Examples of Decision Making and Taking Ownership

There are many real-life examples of individuals who have demonstrated effective decision making and ownership. For instance, entrepreneurs often have to make tough decisions about their businesses and take full responsibility for the outcomes. Leaders in various fields also exemplify these skills, as they are responsible for guiding their teams and organizations towards success.

One example I can offer is when I hire people. Over the years, I've become masterful at this skill. I understand the personality traits of impactful employees. Better still, I know the traits of those who are terrible. So, with this knowledge driving me – I pepper people with questions to reveal both the good and the bad traits. For example: I ask – when was the last time you lost your temper in the office. What happened? Their answers tell me all I need to know about a person. Armed with this information – the decision to hire them or not becomes easy.

In the realm of personal development, individuals who have overcome significant challenges often credit their success to their ability to make decisions and take ownership of their lives. These stories can serve as powerful examples and inspiration for others.

Lessons Learned from Case Studies

Case studies on decision making and taking ownership often reveal common themes. One key lesson is the importance of having a clear vision and set of values to guide decision making. Another lesson is the need for resilience and the ability to bounce back from setbacks.

These case studies also highlight the value of seeking feedback and learning from others. They show that taking ownership doesn't mean going it alone; it often involves collaboration and support from others. Finally, these stories demonstrate that taking risks and stepping out of your comfort zone are essential for growth and success.

Activities for Decision Making and Taking Ownership

Practical Exercises for Decision Making and Taking Ownership

There are several practical exercises that can help you develop your decision making and ownership skills. Role-playing scenarios can provide an opportunity to practice making decisions in a low-risk environment. Writing in a journal can help you reflect on past decisions and take ownership of your actions.

Setting personal goals and creating action plans can also be effective exercises. These activities encourage you to take ownership of your personal development and to make decisions that align with your goals.

Reflective Activities for Decision Making and Taking Ownership

Reflective activities, such as meditation and mindfulness, can help you become more aware of your decision-making process and the role that emotions play in it. Reflecting on your values and how they influence your decisions is another valuable activity.

Seeking feedback from others and reflecting on their perspectives can also enhance your decision making and ownership skills. Reflective activities encourage introspection and self-awareness, which are critical for personal mastery.

Famous Quotes

"The only person you are destined to become is the person you decide to be." - Ralph Waldo Emerson

This quote emphasizes the power of decision-making in shaping our identities. Emerson, a famous American essayist, lecturer, philosopher, and poet, believed that we have the power to decide who we want to be.

"In the end, we only regret the chances we didn't take, relationships we were afraid to have, and the decisions we waited too long to make." - Lewis Carroll

Carroll, the author of "Alice in Wonderland," reminds us of the importance of taking risks and making decisions. His quote encourages us to seize opportunities and not let fear hold us back.

"It's not hard to make decisions when you know what your values are." - Roy Disney

Roy Disney, co-founder of The Walt Disney Company, highlights the importance of knowing your values. When you understand what's important to you, decision-making becomes easier.

"The greatest mistake we make is living in constant fear that we will make one." - John C. Maxwell

John C. Maxwell, a famous leadership expert, emphasizes that making mistakes is a part of life. Instead of fearing them, we should embrace them as learning opportunities.

Decision Making, Ownership and Self-confidence

How Decision Making and Taking Ownership Builds Self-Confidence

Decision making and taking ownership can have a significant impact on self-confidence. When you make decisions, especially difficult ones, and see positive outcomes, it reinforces your belief in your abilities. Taking ownership of your actions and their consequences also builds self-confidence, as it demonstrates your ability to influence your life's direction.

As you become more skilled at making decisions and taking ownership, your self-confidence grows. This increased confidence can then lead to more effective decision making and ownership, creating a positive feedback loop.

The Interplay Between Self-Confidence, Decision Making and Ownership

Self-confidence, decision making, and ownership are closely interconnected. Self-confidence enhances your ability to make decisions and take ownership, as it gives you the courage to take risks and the resilience to deal with the outcomes. In turn, effective decision making and taking ownership can strengthen your self-confidence.

This interplay creates a virtuous cycle that can lead to greater personal mastery. As you become more confident in your abilities, you're more likely to make decisions that align with your goals and values, and to take full ownership of your life's journey.

The Power of Decision Making and Taking Ownership

Reflecting on the Journey of Decision Making and Taking Ownership

Reflecting on the journey of decision making and taking ownership is an important part of personal mastery. It allows you to see how far you've come and to appreciate the progress you've made. It also helps you identify areas where you can continue to grow and improve.

This reflection can be a source of motivation and inspiration, as it reminds you of the power you must shape your life and the positive impact that effective decision making, and ownership can have.

Looking Forward: Decision Making and Ownership in the Journey to Mastery

Looking forward, decision making, and ownership will continue to play a crucial role in your journey to personal mastery. As you face new challenges and opportunities, the skills you've developed will help you navigate them with confidence and purpose.

By continuing to practice effective decision making and taking ownership of your actions, you'll be well-equipped to achieve your goals and to live a life that is true to your values and vision. The journey to mastery is ongoing, and decision making, and ownership are key companions on that journey.

1. What is the role of decision making in personal mastery?

A. It helps to avoid making choices
B. It allows you to take control of your life and actions
C. It is irrelevant to personal mastery
D. It is only important in professional settings

2. Which of the following is NOT a characteristic of effective decision making?

    A. Making a choice and taking action
    B. Evaluating the consequences of each option
    C. Rushing to make a decision
    D. Considering all possible options

3. What does taking ownership in personal mastery involve?

    A. Ignoring the consequences of your actions
    B. Taking responsibility for your actions and their outcomes

    C. Only taking credit for successful outcomes

    D. Blaming others for your mistakes

4. Which of the following is a strategy for overcoming challenges in decision making and taking ownership?

    A. Avoiding difficult decisions
    B. Seeking support and advice when needed
    C. Ignoring the problem
    D. Making impulsive decisions

5. How does decision making and taking ownership contribute to selfconfidence?

    A. It doesn't contribute to self-confidence
    B. It makes you dependent on others
    C. It builds self-confidence by allowing you to trust

your judgment and abilities
D.   It lowers self-confidence by making you question your decisions

16. ADAPTING TO CHANGE

The Importance of Adapting to Change

Benefits of Adapting to Change

Adapting to change is beneficial for several reasons. Firstly, it fosters flexibility and adaptability, qualities that are essential in today's fast paced world. Those who adapt well to change are better equipped to handle the unexpected and can pivot more easily when plans fall through.

Secondly, adapting to change encourages personal growth. When faced with new situations, individuals are pushed out of their comfort zones, which can lead to new skills and insights. Lastly, being adaptable can lead to increased opportunities. Embracing change can open doors to new experiences, relationships, and paths that might otherwise have been missed.

Adapting to Change and Personal Growth

Personal growth is deeply intertwined with one's ability to adapt to change. As teenagers encounter new stages in life, such as transitioning from middle school to high school, they are presented with opportunities to learn more about themselves and the world around them. Adapting to these changes can lead to a deeper understanding of personal values, strengths, and areas for improvement.

Furthermore, adapting to change can help in developing a growth mindset, where challenges are seen as opportunities to grow rather than insurmountable barriers. This mindset is crucial for personal development and achieving success in various aspects of life.

Dweck's research has focused on why people succeed and how to foster success. She has held professorships at Columbia and Harvard Universities, has lectured all over the world, and has been elected to the American Academy of Arts and Sciences.

Her Contribution

Her most notable work, Mindset: The New Psychology of Success, introduces the idea of "mindset" and explains how our perception of ourselves can impact our abilities and outcomes in life. In her book, she discusses the difference between a "fixed" mindset and a "growth" mindset.

> Fixed Mindset: People with a fixed mindset believe their basic abilities, intelligence, and talents are fixed traits. They spend their time documenting their intelligence instead of developing them.

> Growth Mindset: People with a growth mindset believe that their most basic abilities can be developed through dedication and hard work. This view creates a love of learning and resilience that is essential for great accomplishment.

Dweck's work has been influential in shifting attitudes in education and parenting towards encouraging a growth mindset, and her research has been used in a wide variety of settings.

Effective Adaptation to Change

Identifying Characteristics of Effective Adaptation

Effective adaptation to change is characterized by several key traits. One such trait is proactivity, which involves taking initiative and preparing for change rather than simply reacting to it. Another important characteristic is resilience, the ability to recover quickly from difficulties and setbacks.

Optimism is also a hallmark of effective adaptation, as it allows individuals to maintain a positive outlook even in the face of uncertainty. Lastly, resourcefulness is crucial; being able to creatively use available resources to navigate change is a valuable skill.

Steps to Adapting to Change Effectively

Adapting to change effectively involves several steps. The first step is to acknowledge the change, recognizing its presence and impact on one's life. The second step is to assess the situation, understanding what the change entails and what it means for the future.

The third step is to plan a course of action, setting goals and identifying strategies to manage the change. The fourth step is to take action, implementing the plan and making necessary adjustments along the way. Finally, the fifth step is to reflect on the experience, learning from both successes and failures to improve future adaptation efforts.

Maintaining Adaptation Over Time

Maintaining adaptation over time requires continuous effort and selfreflection. It involves staying informed about potential changes and updating one's strategies to cope with them. It also means cultivating a supportive network of friends, family, and mentors who can provide guidance and encouragement.

Additionally, maintaining a journal or other record of one's experiences with change can be helpful for tracking progress and identifying patterns in how one adapts. This ongoing process ensures that the skills and insights gained from adapting to change are not lost but rather built upon for future growth.

1. What does maintaining adaptation over time involve?

2. Why is it important to stay informed about potential changes?

3. How can a supportive network of friends, family, and mentors help in adapting to change?

4. What is the role of a journal in maintaining adaptation over time?

5. How does the ongoing process of adaptation ensure future growth?

Reflect on these questions and jot down your answers. Compare them with the content in the chapter to see how well you've grasped the concept. Remember, understanding is the first step towards mastery!

Overcoming Challenges in Adapting to Change

Identifying Challenges

Overcoming challenges in adapting to change begins with identifying them. Common challenges include fear of the unknown, which can paralyze decision-making, and resistance to change, which can stem from a desire to maintain the status quo. Other challenges include emotional responses such as anxiety or sadness, and practical concerns like lack of resources or support.

Strategies for Overcoming Challenges

Strategies for overcoming these challenges include educating oneself about the change, which can reduce fear and uncertainty. Building a support network can provide emotional and practical assistance.
Developing coping skills, such as stress management techniques, can help manage emotional responses. Lastly, incremental change, taking small steps towards adaptation, can make the process more manageable.

Seeking Support for Challenges

Seeking support is a critical aspect of overcoming challenges in adapting to change. This support can come from various sources, including family and friends, who can offer emotional support and practical advice. Mentors or counselors can provide guidance and perspective, while peer groups can offer solidarity and shared experiences. Utilizing these resources can make the process of adapting to change less daunting and more successful.

The Role of Change in Stress Management

Understanding Stress Management

Stress management is the practice of using strategies to reduce or handle the pressures of life. It involves recognizing stressors, understanding how they affect us, and learning techniques to mitigate their impact. Effective stress management can lead to improved mental and physical health, as well as increased productivity and happiness.

Change and Stress Management

Change is often a significant source of stress, but it can also play a role in stress management. Adapting to change can teach us how to deal with uncertainty and develop coping mechanisms that can be applied to other stressful situations. By learning to navigate change, we can become more resilient and better equipped to handle future stressors.

Managing Stress through Adaptation

Managing stress through adaptation involves several key strategies. One strategy is to maintain a routine where possible, as familiarity can provide comfort during times of change. Another strategy is to practice mindfulness and relaxation techniques, which can help calm the mind and reduce anxiety. Additionally, physical activity and healthy eating can improve one's ability to cope with stress. Lastly, seeking professional help when needed can provide additional support and resources for managing stress.

Case Studies on Adapting to Change

Real-Life Examples of Adapting to Change

Real-life examples of adapting to change can provide valuable insights and inspiration. For instance, the story of a teenager who moves to a new country and learns a new language shows the power of resilience and determination. Another example might be a student who overcomes a learning disability by developing new study strategies, demonstrating adaptability and resourcefulness.

Lessons Learned from Case Studies

From these case studies, we can learn that adapting to change often requires a combination of inner strength and external support. We also see that while change can be challenging, it can lead to personal growth and new opportunities. These stories can serve as a reminder that everyone faces change and that success in adaptation is possible with the right mindset and tools.

Activities for Adapting to Change

Practical Exercises for Adapting to Change

Practical exercises for adapting to change can help teenagers develop the skills they need to navigate life's transitions. Activities such as role-playing different scenarios can prepare them for real-life situations. Problem-solving games can enhance their ability to think on their feet. Additionally, goal-setting workshops can teach them how to plan for and adapt to future changes.

Reflective Activities for Adapting to Change

Reflective activities, such as journaling about experiences with change, can provide personal insights and help track progress. Meditation and mindfulness exercises can foster a calm and focused mindset, aiding in adaptation. Group discussions about change can also offer support and shared learning opportunities.

Think & Reflect

Change is a constant part of life, and how we adapt to it can greatly affect our personal growth and development. Here are some questions to ponder on:

1. Think about a recent change in your life. How did you feel about it? What were the challenges and how did you overcome them?

2. How do you usually react to change? Do you embrace it, resist it, or feel indifferent about it?

3. Reflect on a time when you resisted change. What were the reasons? In hindsight, would you have reacted differently?

4. Consider a change you're currently facing. How can you apply mindfulness and meditation to better adapt to this change?

5. Imagine a future change that could occur in your life. How can you prepare for it mentally and emotionally?

Remember, reflecting on these questions is not about finding right or wrong answers. It's about gaining deeper understanding of your own reactions to change, and finding ways to adapt more effectively in the future.

Adapting to Change and Self-Confidence

How Adapting to Change Builds Self-Confidence

Adapting to change can significantly build self-confidence. Successfully navigating a challenging situation can lead to a sense of accomplishment and a belief in one's abilities. This increased self-confidence can then empower teenagers to take on new challenges and step out of their comfort zones with greater assurance.

The Interplay Between Self-Confidence and Adaptation

There is a dynamic interplay between self-confidence and adaptation. As individuals become more confident in their ability to adapt, they are more likely to embrace change rather than fear it. Conversely, as they become more adept at adapting to change, their self-confidence grows. This positive feedback loop can lead to a virtuous cycle of growth and development.

Adapting to Change and Goal Achievement

The Role of Adaptation in Achieving Goals

Adaptation plays a crucial role in achieving goals. Goals often require change, whether it's developing new habits, learning new skills, or changing one's environment. Being able to adapt to these changes is essential for reaching one's goals. It allows for flexibility in the face of obstacles and the ability to adjust one's approach as needed.

Adapting to Change for Goal Achievement

To use adaptation for goal achievement, it's important to set realistic and flexible goals that can accommodate change. It's also helpful to develop a plan B for when the original plan is disrupted by change. Celebrating small victories along the way can maintain motivation and reinforce the ability to adapt.

The Power of Adapting to Change

Reflecting on the Journey of Adapting to Change

Reflecting on the journey of adapting to change is an important part of personal mastery. It allows individuals to recognize their growth, appreciate their resilience, and learn from their experiences. This reflection can also provide valuable lessons for future changes and challenges.

Looking Forward: Adapting to Change in the Journey to Mastery

Looking forward, adapting to change will continue to be an integral part of the journey to mastery. As teenagers grow and evolve, they will face new changes and transitions. By applying the skills and knowledge they have gained, they can approach these changes with confidence and a sense of purpose, knowing that each change is an opportunity to move closer to their full potential.

1. What is the role of change in personal mastery?

    A. Change is a hindrance to personal mastery.
    B. Change is irrelevant to personal mastery.
    C. Change is an integral part of personal mastery.
    D. Change undermines personal mastery.

2. Which of the following is NOT a benefit of adapting to change?

    A. Increased resilience
    B. Improved stress management
    C. Enhanced self-confidence
    D. Stagnation and lack of growth

3. What is one of the steps to adapting to change effectively?

    A. Identifying the change and its impact
    B. Resisting the change
    C. Avoiding the change
    D. Ignoring the change

4. How does adapting to change build self-confidence?

    A. Adapting to change builds self-confidence by eliminating all challenges.
    B. Adapting to change decreases self-confidence because it involves facing uncertainty.
    C. By successfully adapting to change, individuals gain confidence in their abilities to handle new situations.
    D. It doesn't. Adapting to change and self-confidence are unrelated.

5. What is the role of adaptation in achieving goals?

    A. Adaptation changes the goals themselves, making them easier to achieve.
    B. Adaptation is not necessary for achieving goals.
    C. Adaptation distracts individuals from their goals.
    D. Adaptation can help individuals adjust their strategies to overcome obstacles and achieve their goals.

17. BUILDING A SUPPORT SYSTEM

Understanding a Support System

What is a Support System?

A support system is a network of people who provide an individual with practical or emotional support. It's made up of friends, family, teachers, mentors, and sometimes even peers who can offer advice, guidance, and a listening ear when needed. A support system can be seen as a safety net that catches us when we fall and helps us to climb back up to face the challenges of life.

Support systems are not one-size-fits-all; they are unique to each person and can vary greatly in size and function. Some people may have a large group of friends and family to lean on, while others might find support through online communities or a small circle of close acquaintances. The key is that these individuals or groups are sources of positive reinforcement, encouragement, and assistance.

The Role of a Support System in Personal Mastery

Personal mastery is about having a deep understanding of oneself and a commitment to personal growth. It involves setting goals, overcoming obstacles, and achieving one's highest potential. A support system plays a crucial role in this journey by providing guidance, motivation, and accountability. When pursuing personal mastery, it's easy to become discouraged or lose sight of one's goals. A support system helps to keep an individual focused and on track.

Moreover, a support system can offer different perspectives and insights that might be overlooked by the individual. It can challenge one's thinking, provide constructive feedback, and encourage taking risks that lead to personal growth. In essence, a support system is a vital component in the toolkit of anyone seeking to master themselves and their life.

The Importance of a Support System

Benefits of a Support System

The benefits of having a support system are numerous. It can lead to better stress management, as having people to talk to can reduce feelings of anxiety and depression. A support system can also improve one's physical health; studies have shown that people with strong social ties have a lower risk of disease and a higher chance of survival after a heart attack.

Furthermore, a support system can boost self-esteem and confidence. Knowing that there are people who believe in you and your abilities can make you feel more secure in your decisions and more willing to take on new challenges. It can also provide a sense of belonging, which is essential for mental and emotional well-being.

Support System and Personal Growth

A support system is not just there for the tough times; it's also there to celebrate successes and milestones. This positive reinforcement can encourage further personal growth and development. Additionally, a support system can serve as a sounding board for ideas and dreams, helping to refine them and turn them into actionable goals.

Personal growth often involves stepping out of one's comfort zone, which can be daunting. A support system provides the encouragement and backup needed to take these steps. It can also offer practical help, such as assistance with tasks or sharing of resources, which can be invaluable when pursuing new ventures or learning new skills.

Building an Effective Support System

Identifying Characteristics of an Effective Support

System

An effective support system is characterized by trust, mutual respect, and open communication. It should consist of individuals who are positive, supportive, and willing to provide honest feedback when necessary. Diversity within a support system is also beneficial, as it brings a range of perspectives and experiences that can aid in problem-solving and decision-making.

Another important characteristic is reliability. Members of a support system should be dependable and consistent in their support. This creates a stable environment where an individual feels safe to share their thoughts and feelings without fear of judgment or abandonment.

Steps to Building a Support System

Building a support system takes time and effort. It starts with identifying the qualities you value in a supporter and seeking out individuals who embody those qualities. This can be done through joining clubs, groups, or organizations where you can meet like-minded people. It's also important to be proactive in reaching out and building relationships. This might involve asking someone to be a mentor, joining a study group, or simply spending more time with family and friends.

Another step is to be a good supporter yourself. Being there for others can encourage them to reciprocate. It's also crucial to communicate your needs to your support system; people can't help if they don't know what you need. Lastly, it's important to evaluate and adjust your support system as needed. As you grow and change, your support needs may also change, and your support system should reflect that.

Maintaining a Support System Over Time

Maintaining a support system requires regular communication and nurturing of relationships. This might involve scheduling regular check-ins, sharing updates on your life, and being there for others in their times of need. It's also important to show appreciation for your support system; a simple thank you can go a long way in maintaining strong relationships.

Conflicts and misunderstandings can occur in any relationship, and it's important to address these issues promptly and constructively. Keeping a support system strong also means being willing to let go of relationships that are no longer supportive or healthy. This can be difficult, but it's sometimes necessary to make room for more positive influences in your life.

Overcoming Challenges in Building a Support System

Identifying Challenges

One of the challenges in building a support system is the fear of rejection. It can be intimidating to reach out to others and ask for support. There's also the challenge of finding the right people who share your values and goals. In some cases, geographical distance can make it difficult to maintain a support system, especially if your supporters are not located nearby.

Another challenge is the time and effort required to build and maintain relationships. With busy schedules and competing priorities, it can be hard to find the time to nurture a support system. Additionally, some individuals may have had negative experiences in the past that make them hesitant to trust others and open up.

Strategies for Overcoming Challenges

To overcome these challenges, it's important to start small. You don't need many people in your support system; a few good supporters can make a significant difference. It's also helpful to practice vulnerability in a safe environment, perhaps by sharing small concerns before moving on to bigger issues.

Utilizing technology can help overcome geographical barriers. Regular video calls, messaging, and social media can keep you connected with your support system no matter where they are. Time management strategies, such as setting aside specific times for social activities, can help ensure that you're investing in your relationships.

Seeking Support for Challenges

If you're struggling to build a support system, don't be afraid to seek help. This could involve talking to a counselor, coach, or trusted advisor who can provide guidance on how to create and maintain supportive relationships. There are also books, workshops, and online resources that can offer tips and strategies for building a support system.

Remember that building a support system is a process, and it's okay to ask for help along the way. Everyone needs support at some point, and seeking assistance is a sign of strength, not weakness.

Further Reading

Expand your knowledge and understanding of building a support system with these recommended books and online resources:

1. "The Art of Asking: How I Learned to Stop Worrying

and Let People Help" by Amanda Palmer. This book explores the concept of asking for help and how it can strengthen your support system.

2. "Give and Take: Why Helping Others Drives Our Success" by Adam Grant. This book provides insights into the importance of giving and receiving support.

3. "The Power of Two: Secrets to a Strong & Loving Marriage" by Susan Heitler. Although focused on marriage, this book offers valuable insights into building and maintaining supportive relationships.

4. www.mindtools.com - This website offers a wealth of resources on personal development, including articles and tools for building a strong support system.

5. www.psychologytoday.com - This website provides numerous articles on the psychology of relationships and support systems.

Remember, seeking help and learning from others is a sign of strength. These resources can provide you with valuable strategies and insights to help you build a strong support system.

The Role of a Support System in Stress Management

Understanding Stress Management

Stress management involves techniques and strategies to handle stress in a healthy way. It's about knowing what triggers your stress and having tools to cope with it. Effective stress management can lead to improved health, mood, productivity, and overall quality of life.

Stress can be caused by a variety of factors, including school pressures, family issues, social dynamics, and personal challenges. Learning to manage stress is a critical skill for personal mastery and can be greatly aided by a strong support system.

Support System and Stress Management

A support system can play a key role in stress management by providing emotional support, practical help, and a different perspective on stressful situations. Talking to someone about your stress can help you process your emotions and come up with solutions. Supporters can also help by taking on some of your tasks, giving you time to relax and recharge.

Moreover, supporters can encourage you to engage in healthy stressreducing activities, such as exercise, hobbies, or relaxation techniques. They can join you in these activities, making them more enjoyable and ensuring that you take the time to do them.

Managing Stress through a Support System

To effectively manage stress through your support system, it's important to communicate openly about what you're experiencing. Let your supporters know what kind of help you need, whether it's a listening ear, advice, or assistance with specific tasks. It's also helpful to establish boundaries so that your supporters know when and how they can best assist you.

Engaging in group stress-reducing activities, such as group exercise classes or meditation sessions, can also be beneficial. These activities not only help manage stress but also strengthen the bonds within your support system.

Think & Reflect

Consider Your Own Support System

Take a moment to think about your own support system. Who are the people you can rely on when you're feeling stressed or overwhelmed?

This could be family, friends, teachers, or even online communities.

Write down their names and how they can help you manage stress.

Who are the people in your support system?

What kind of help can they provide?

How can you communicate your needs to them effectively?

Group Activities for Stress Management

Now, think about some group activities that you and your support system can engage in to manage stress. These could be physical activities like sports or yoga, or they could be more relaxed activities like watching a movie together or having a group study session. Write down a few ideas and discuss them with your support system.

Case Studies on Building a Support System

Real-Life Examples of Building a Support System

There are many inspiring stories of individuals who have successfully built strong support systems. For example, a teenager who moved to a new city and felt isolated at school might start a study group to meet new friends. Over time, this group could evolve into a supportive network that helps each member with academic and personal challenges.

Another example could be a young athlete who relies on their coach, teammates, and family to overcome performance anxiety and injuries. Their support system provides encouragement, advice on recovery, and motivation to keep striving for their goals.

Lessons Learned from Case Studies

From these case studies, we can learn that building a support system often requires taking initiative and being open to new relationships. It's also clear that support systems can come from a variety of sources, not just traditional ones like family and friends. Additionally, these stories show that a support system can evolve and grow over time, adapting to the changing needs of the individual.

Another important lesson is that the quality of support is more important than the quantity. Having a few reliable and trustworthy supporters is often more beneficial than having a large number of acquaintances.

Activities for Building a Support System

Practical Exercises for Building a Support System

There are several practical exercises that can help you build a support system. One exercise is to make a list of qualities you value in a supporter and then identify people in your life who embody those qualities. Another exercise is to set a goal to reach out to one new person each week, whether it's striking up a conversation with a classmate or asking a teacher for advice.

Group activities, such as joining a club or sports team, can also be a great way to meet potential supporters. Volunteering is another excellent way to build relationships while giving back to the community.

Reflective Activities for Building a Support System

Reflective activities can also aid in building a support system. Journaling about your experiences with support can help you understand what works for you and what doesn't. Reflecting on past relationships can provide insights into the characteristics of a good supporter and any patterns that may be hindering your ability to build a strong support system.

Meditation and mindfulness can help you become more aware of your needs and the type of support that would be most beneficial to you. They can also help you develop the confidence and communication skills needed to build and maintain supportive relationships.

Support System and Self-Confidence

How a Support System Builds Self-Confidence

A support system can significantly boost self-confidence by

providing positive feedback, encouragement, and validation. When you know that others believe in you, it's easier to believe in yourself. Supporters can also help you recognize your strengths and achievements, which can increase your self-confidence.

Additionally, a support system can provide a safe space to try new things and take risks. Knowing that you have people to fall back on if things don't go as planned can give you the courage to step out of your comfort zone and build confidence through new experiences.

The Interplay Between Self-Confidence and a Support System

The relationship between self-confidence and a support system is reciprocal. As your self-confidence grows, you're more likely to seek out and maintain supportive relationships. Conversely, a strong support system can foster further growth in self-confidence.

It's important to nurture both your self-confidence and your support system, as they can reinforce and strengthen each other. A confident individual is more likely to attract supportive people, and a supportive environment can help an individual become more confident.

Support System and Goal Achievement

The Role of a Support System in Achieving Goals

A support system can play a critical role in achieving goals by providing motivation, resources, and accountability. Supporters can remind you of your goals and why they're important, especially when you're facing obstacles or feeling discouraged.

They can also offer practical help, such as assisting with tasks or sharing knowledge and expertise. Additionally, having someone to be accountable to can increase your commitment to your goals and the likelihood of achieving them.

Building a Support System for Goal Achievement

To build a support system for goal achievement, it's important to communicate your goals to your supporters. This allows them to understand how they can best support you. It's also helpful to seek out individuals who have achieved similar goals or who have expertise in areas related to your goals.

Creating a goal-oriented group, such as a study group or a mastermind group, can also be beneficial. These groups can provide a structured environment for sharing progress, challenges, and strategies for achieving goals.

The Power of a Support System

Building a Support System

Reflecting on the journey of building a support system can provide valuable insights into what has worked well and what can be improved. It's an opportunity to recognize the effort you've put into creating supportive relationships and to appreciate the people who have been there for you.

It's also a chance to consider how your support system has evolved and how it has contributed to your personal growth and mastery. Reflection can help you identify any gaps in your support system and plan for how to fill them.

Looking Forward: Support System in the Journey to

Mastery

Looking forward, a support system will continue to be an essential part of the journey to personal mastery. As you set new goals and face new challenges, your support system will provide the stability and encouragement needed to keep moving forward.

Continuing to invest in your support system, being open to new relationships, and being a supportive presence in the lives of others will ensure that your support system remains strong and effective. The power of a support system lies in its ability to lift you up and propel you toward your highest potential.

18. RESPECTING YOURSELF AND OTHERS

Understanding Respect

What is Respect?

Respect is a fundamental value that signifies the appreciation and consideration we have for ourselves and others. It involves recognizing the worth and dignity of every person, including oneself, and acting in ways that demonstrate this recognition. Respect is not just about polite actions or words; it's an attitude that influences how we interact with people and the world around us. It encompasses listening actively, valuing opinions, and treating others with kindness and fairness.

In the context of self-improvement, respect is a two-way street. It's not only about how we treat others but also how we treat ourselves. Self-respect is the cornerstone of personal dignity and integrity, while respecting others fosters positive relationships and a supportive community. When we practice respect consistently, it becomes a part of our character, shaping our interactions and helping us to navigate the social world with grace and empathy.

The Role of Respect in Personal Mastery

Respect plays a crucial role in personal mastery, which is the ongoing process of self-improvement and self-discovery. When we respect ourselves, we are more likely to set healthy boundaries, pursue our goals, and maintain a positive self-image. This self-respect also empowers us to demand respect from others, creating a cycle of positive reinforcement that elevates our sense of self-worth.

Conversely, when we respect others, we open ourselves up to diverse perspectives and experiences that can enrich our understanding of the world. This can lead to improved communication, stronger relationships, and a deeper sense of community. In essence, respect is the foundation upon which personal mastery is built, as it encourages us to grow and learn in a way that honors both ourselves and those around us.

Further Reading

Interested in learning more about respect and personal mastery? Here are some recommended books that can help you deepen your understanding:

"The Respect Principle: Connecting with Others through the Power of Respect" by Dr. Richard L. Evans - This book explores the concept of respect in depth, providing practical strategies for cultivating respect in your daily life.

"The Mastery of Love: A Practical Guide to the Art ofRelationship" by Don Miguel Ruiz - This book offers insights into the role of respect in relationships and how it contributes to personal mastery.

Remember, reading is a great way to expand your knowledge and understanding. So, dive in and discover more about the power of respect!

The Importance of Self-Respect

Benefits of Self-Respect

Self-respect is integral to our overall well-being and happiness. It affects how we see ourselves and how we choose to navigate life's challenges. With self-respect, we are more likely to make choices that align with our values and to stand up for ourselves in difficult situations. It also fosters resilience, as we are better equipped to bounce back from setbacks when we believe in our own worth.

Additionally, self-respect can lead to healthier relationships. When we value ourselves, we set a standard for how we expect to be treated by others. This can deter negative relationships and attract those who will honor our self-worth. Moreover, self-respect can improve our performance in various areas of life, such as school and work, because it motivates us to put forth our best effort and to take pride in our accomplishments.

Self-Respect and Personal Growth

Self-respect is a driving force behind personal growth. It encourages us to pursue our interests and passions, even in the face of adversity. With self-respect, we are more likely to take risks and step out of our comfort zones, which are essential steps in the journey of self-improvement. It also helps us to accept and learn from our mistakes, rather than letting them diminish our self-worth.

Furthermore, self-respect is key to developing self-discipline and accountability. When we respect ourselves, we hold ourselves to high standards and are more committed to our personal goals. This sense of responsibility can lead to significant achievements and a fulfilling life. In essence, self-respect is not just about feeling good about ourselves; it's about creating a life that reflects our highest potential.

Cultivating Self-Respect

Identifying Characteristics of Self-Respect

Self-respect is characterized by several key attributes. It involves recognizing our intrinsic value, treating ourselves with kindness, and not compromising our beliefs or values for the sake of others' approval. It also means taking care of our physical and emotional well-being, setting boundaries, and being assertive when necessary.

Another characteristic of self-respect is the ability to forgive ourselves. We all make mistakes, but those with self-respect understand that errors do not define their worth. They learn from these experiences and move forward with a renewed commitment to their values. Additionally, self-respect involves celebrating our achievements, no matter how small, and recognizing our progress in life.

Steps to Cultivating Self-Respect

Cultivating self-respect is a process that requires intention and effort. The first step is to engage in self-reflection to understand our values and beliefs. Once we have a clear sense of what is important to us, we can begin to align our actions with these values. This might involve making changes in our lives, such as ending toxic relationships or pursuing new opportunities that reflect our self-worth.

Another step is to practice self-care. This includes taking care of our physical health through exercise and nutrition, as well as our mental health through activities like meditation or therapy. Self-care reinforces the idea that we are worthy of time and attention. Additionally, setting and achieving goals can build self-respect, as it shows us that we can make positive changes in our lives.

Maintaining Self-Respect Over Time

Maintaining self-respect over time requires ongoing attention and commitment. It's important to regularly check in with ourselves to ensure that our actions continue to align with our values. This might involve periodic self-reflection or journaling to monitor our progress and challenges.

It's also crucial to surround ourselves with people who respect us and support our journey. These individuals can provide encouragement and feedback that help us stay on track. Lastly, we must be willing to adapt and grow as we encounter new experiences and information. By staying open to learning and evolving, we can maintain a strong sense of self-respect throughout our lives.

The Importance of Respecting Others

Benefits of Respecting Others

Respecting others has numerous benefits for both individuals and society. When we show respect to others, we create a positive and inclusive environment that encourages cooperation and harmony. This can lead to more effective teamwork, better communication, and stronger communities.

Additionally, respecting others can enhance our own personal development. It exposes us to different perspectives and ideas, which can broaden our understanding and empathy. By valuing others' experiences, we can learn new skills and gain insights that contribute to our growth. Respect for others also fosters trust and openness, which are essential for building meaningful relationships.

Respecting Others and Personal Growth

Respecting others is a vital component of personal growth. It teaches us to appreciate diversity and to recognize the value in everyone's unique contributions. This respect can lead to a deeper sense of connection with those around us, which can be incredibly fulfilling.

Moreover, when we respect others, we are more likely to be respected in return. This mutual respect can create a supportive network that encourages us to pursue our goals and overcome obstacles. It also helps us to develop important social skills, such as active listening and conflict resolution, which are valuable in all areas of life.

Cultivating Respect for Others
Identifying Characteristics of Respect for Others

Respect for others is characterized by behaviors such as active listening, empathy, and consideration. It involves acknowledging others' feelings, thoughts, and experiences as valid and important. It also means treating people with courtesy and politeness, regardless of their background or status.

Another characteristic of respect for others is the willingness to learn from them. This includes being open to feedback and different viewpoints, as well as recognizing the value of collaboration. Additionally, respect for others involves advocating for fairness and justice, and standing up against discrimination and prejudice.

Steps to Cultivating Respect for Others

Cultivating respect for others begins with self-awareness. We must be mindful of our biases and prejudices and actively work to overcome them. This can involve educating ourselves about different cultures and experiences, as well as engaging in conversations with people who have different perspectives.

Another step is to practice empathy. This means putting ourselves in others' shoes and trying to understand their feelings and experiences. We can also demonstrate respect by being reliable and keeping our promises, as well as by giving credit where it's due. Lastly, we should strive to treat everyone with kindness and compassion, regardless of how they treat us.

Maintaining Respect for Others Over Time

Maintaining respect for others over time requires continuous effort and reflection. It's important to remain open to learning and to challenge our own assumptions and stereotypes. We should also seek out diverse experiences and relationships that can expand our understanding and empathy.

Additionally, we can maintain respect for others by being consistent in our respectful behavior. This means treating everyone with courtesy and kindness, even in challenging situations. We can also support initiatives and organizations that promote respect and inclusion. By making respect for others a core part of our values, we can ensure that it remains a guiding principle in our lives.

Overcoming Challenges in Respecting Yourself and Others

Identifying Challenges

One of the challenges in respecting ourselves and others is dealing with societal pressures and stereotypes that can influence our thoughts and actions. We may also face personal insecurities or past experiences that make it difficult to maintain self-respect or respect for others.

Additionally, we may encounter individuals or situations that test our commitment to respect. This could include facing disrespect from others, navigating conflicts, or dealing with rejection. These challenges can be disheartening, but they are also opportunities for growth and learning.

Strategies for Overcoming Challenges

To overcome challenges in respecting ourselves and others, we can employ several strategies. One approach is to reaffirm our values and remind ourselves of the importance of respect. We can also seek support from trusted friends, family, or mentors who can provide guidance and encouragement.

Another strategy is to practice self-care and self-compassion, which can help us to maintain self-respect in the face of adversity. When it comes to respecting others, we can focus on finding common ground and understanding, even when we disagree. It's also helpful to set boundaries and to communicate clearly and assertively.

Seeking Support for Challenges

Seeking support is an important part of overcoming challenges in respecting ourselves and others. This can include talking to a counselor or therapist, joining a support group, or participating in workshops and seminars that focus on respect and personal development.

We can also find support in literature, online resources, and community programs that provide tools and strategies for building respect. By reaching out for help, we can gain new perspectives and strategies that empower us to overcome obstacles and maintain our commitment to respect.

Case Studies on Respecting Yourself and Others

Real-Life Examples of Respecting Yourself and Others

There are many inspiring real-life examples of individuals who have demonstrated respect for themselves and others. These stories can serve as powerful illustrations of the impact that respect can have on our lives and the lives of those around us.

For instance, consider the story of a young person who overcame bullying by cultivating self-respect and assertiveness. Or the tale of a community leader who brought people together by fostering mutual respect and understanding among diverse groups. These case studies highlight the transformative power of respect and how it can lead to positive change.

Lessons Learned from Case Studies

From these case studies, we can learn several important lessons. One is that respect can be a powerful tool for overcoming adversity and building stronger communities. We also see that respect starts with the individual and can ripple out to influence others in profound ways.

Additionally, these stories teach us that cultivating respect requires courage and persistence. It's not always easy, but the rewards are well worth the effort. By learning from these examples, we can be inspired to practice respect in our own lives and to make a positive impact on the world around us.

Activities for Respecting Yourself and Others

Practical Exercises for Respecting Yourself and Others

There are many practical exercises that can help us to cultivate respect for ourselves and others. For example, we can engage in role-playing

activities that allow us to practice assertiveness and empathy. We can also participate in group discussions that explore different aspects of respect and how to apply them in real-life situations.

Another exercise is to create a "respect journal" where we record acts of respect that we observe or participate in each day. This can help us to become more aware of respect in our daily lives and to recognize opportunities to practice it.

Reflective Activities for Respecting Yourself and Others

Reflective activities can also be beneficial in cultivating respect. This might include meditation or mindfulness practices that focus on self compassion and understanding. We can also reflect on our interactions with others and consider how we might show more respect in the future.

Writing letters of gratitude to ourselves or others is another reflective activity that can reinforce the importance of respect.

By taking the time to acknowledge and appreciate the value of ourselves and others, we can deepen our commitment to respect.

Respect, Self-Confidence and Self-Esteem

How Respect Builds Self-Confidence and Self-Esteem

Respect is closely linked to self-confidence and self-esteem. When we respect ourselves, we are affirming our worth and capabilities, which can boost our confidence and self-esteem. This, in turn, can lead us to take on new challenges and to believe in our ability to succeed.

Similarly, when we respect others, we are often met with respect in return. This mutual respect can reinforce our positive self-image and encourage us to continue growing and developing. By fostering respect in our relationships, we can create a supportive environment that nurtures self-confidence and self-esteem.

The Interplay Between Self-Confidence, Self-Esteem and Respect

The interplay between self-confidence, self-esteem, and respect is dynamic and reciprocal. As our self-confidence and self-esteem grow, we are more likely to act with respect towards ourselves and others.
Conversely, practicing respect can strengthen our self-confidence and self-esteem.

This interplay creates a positive feedback loop that can lead to significant personal growth. By understanding and leveraging this relationship, we can enhance our journey towards personal mastery and a fulfilling life.

"To be yourself in a world that is constantly trying to make you something else is the greatest accomplishment." - Ralph Waldo Emerson

Ralph Waldo Emerson, a famous American essayist, highlights the importance of maintaining our individuality and self-respect amidst societal pressures.

The Power of Respecting Yourself and Others

Reflecting on the Journey of Respecting Yourself and
Others

As we reflect on the journey of respecting ourselves and others, we can see how this value has shaped our experiences and relationships. Respect is more than just a moral imperative; it's a practical tool that can help us to navigate life with dignity and grace.

By committing to respect, we can create a life that is rich in meaning and connection. We can also inspire others to do the same, contributing to a more respectful and compassionate world.

Looking Forward: Respecting Yourself and Others in the
Journey to Mastery

Looking forward, respect will continue to be an essential part of our journey to personal mastery. It will guide our interactions, influence our choices, and shape our path towards growth and fulfillment.

As we continue to develop and refine our understanding of respect, we can look forward to a future that is characterized by self-confidence, strong relationships, and a deep sense of self-worth. The power of respecting ourselves and others is limitless, and it is a journey that is well worth pursuing.

1. What is one of the benefits of self-respect?

    A. It contributes to personal growth.

B. It makes you immune to criticism.
   C. It makes you more popular.
   D. It guarantees success in life.

2. Which of the following is a step to cultivating self-respect?

   A. Identifying your strengths and weaknesses.
   B. Ignoring your feelings and emotions.
   C. Always putting others' needs before your own.
   D. Comparing yourself to others.

3. How does respecting others contribute to personal growth?

   A. It makes you more attractive to others.
   B. It helps you make more friends.
   C. It increases your understanding and empathy.

   D. It ensures that others will always agree with you.

4. What is a strategy for overcoming challenges in respecting yourself and others?

   A. Ignoring the problem.
   B. Seeking support and guidance.
   C. Blaming others for your feelings.
   D. Avoiding people who are different from you.

5. How does respect contribute to self-confidence and self-esteem?

   A. It makes you more popular, which boosts your self-esteem.
   B. It helps you understand and value your own worth, which builds self-confidence.
   C. It makes you immune to criticism, which boosts your self-esteem.

D. It ensures that others will always agree with you, which increases your self-confidence.

19. CELEBRATING GROWTH AND PROGRESS

Understanding Growth and Progress

What is Growth and Progress?

Growth and progress are fundamental concepts in the journey of personal mastery. Growth refers to the process of developing or maturing physically, mentally, emotionally, or spiritually. It is the expansion of one's abilities, knowledge, and personal attributes. Progress, on the other hand, is the forward or onward movement towards a destination or a more advanced state. It is often measured by the achievement of goals and overcoming obstacles that once stood in the way.

Together, growth and progress represent the continuous journey of improvement and the pursuit of reaching one's full potential. This journey is not linear; it involves setbacks and challenges, but also learning and development. Recognizing and understanding the nuances of growth and progress are essential for teenagers as they navigate through various stages of their lives.

The Role of Growth and Progress in Personal Mastery

In the context of personal mastery, growth and progress are the benchmarks that indicate how far an individual has come in their development. Personal mastery is about self-discovery, self-improvement, and ultimately, self-fulfillment. It is a lifelong process that involves setting personal standards, striving towards them, and then setting new, higher standards.

The role of growth and progress in personal mastery is twofold. Firstly, they serve as motivators, encouraging individuals to continue pushing their boundaries and striving for excellence. Secondly, they act as indicators of success, providing tangible evidence that efforts and strategies are effective. This recognition of growth and progress is crucial for maintaining motivation and commitment to personal mastery.

> A study by the American Journal of Education found that students who recognized their own growth and progress were more likely to stay motivated and engaged in their learning.

The Importance of Celebrating Growth and Progress

Benefits of Celebrating Growth and Progress

Celebrating growth and progress has numerous benefits. It reinforces positive behavior, boosts morale, and provides a sense of accomplishment. When teenagers celebrate their achievements, they experience a release of dopamine, a neurotransmitter associated with feelings of pleasure and satisfaction. This positive reinforcement encourages them to continue their efforts and take on new challenges.

Additionally, celebrating achievements helps to build a positive self-image and self-worth. It allows teenagers to reflect on their journey, acknowledge the hard work they have put in, and recognize their ability to overcome obstacles. This recognition is vital for building resilience and a growth mindset, which are key components of personal mastery.

Celebrating Growth and Progress and Personal Growth

The act of celebrating growth and progress is not just about acknowledging success; it is also about personal growth. It provides an opportunity for self-reflection, helping individuals to understand what strategies worked, what didn't, and how they can improve in the future. This reflective practice is a cornerstone of personal mastery, as it leads to greater self-awareness and insight.

Furthermore, celebrating growth and progress can inspire others. When teenagers share their successes, they can motivate their peers to pursue their own goals and embrace the journey of personal mastery. This collective celebration of growth fosters a supportive community where everyone is encouraged to achieve their best.

Ways to Celebrate Growth and Progress

Identifying Milestones

Identifying milestones is the first step in celebrating growth and progress. Milestones are significant points along the journey that represent important achievements or turning points. They can be as simple as completing a challenging assignment, or as significant as overcoming a personal fear.

To identify milestones, teenagers should set clear, measurable goals at the outset of their endeavors. As they work towards these goals, they should take note of the smaller accomplishments that lead up to the larger goal. These smaller achievements are the milestones that pave the way to success and deserve recognition.

Creating Celebration Rituals

Celebration rituals are personalized activities or traditions that mark the achievement of milestones. They can be private or shared with friends and family. The key is to create a ritual that is meaningful and reflects the significance of the accomplishment.

Some examples of celebration rituals include writing a journal entry, sharing the achievement on social media, having a special meal, or participating in a favorite activity. The ritual should be a deliberate act that honors the hard work and dedication that led to the milestone.

Maintaining Celebration Over Time

Maintaining celebration over time is crucial for sustaining motivation and engagement in the journey to personal mastery. Celebrations should not be reserved for only the largest achievements but should be a regular part of recognizing growth and progress.

To maintain celebration over time, teenagers can create a "success portfolio" where they keep a record of all their achievements, big and small. This portfolio can include certificates, photographs, journal entries, or any other mementos that remind them of their journey. Regularly reviewing this portfolio can provide a boost of confidence and a reminder of how far they have come.

Overcoming Challenges in Celebrating Growth and Progress

Identifying Challenges

One of the challenges in celebrating growth and progress is the tendency to downplay achievements. Teenagers may feel that their accomplishments are not significant enough to warrant celebration, or they may compare themselves to others and feel inadequate.

Another challenge is the lack of recognition from others. Sometimes, the people around may not understand the significance of an achievement or may not provide the encouragement and support that is needed.

Strategies for Overcoming Challenges

To overcome these challenges, it is important to develop a strong sense of self-validation. Teenagers should learn to recognize their own achievements and give themselves credit where it is due. They can also seek out supportive communities or mentors who understand their goals and can provide the recognition and encouragement they need.

Additionally, setting personal standards and measuring progress against those, rather than comparing to others, can help in overcoming the challenge of feeling inadequate. Each individual's journey is unique, and progress should be measured on a personal scale.

Seeking Support for Challenges

Seeking support from friends, family, or mentors can be invaluable when facing challenges in celebrating growth and progress. These individuals can provide a different perspective, help to recognize achievements that may have been overlooked, and offer encouragement to continue on the path of personal mastery.

Support groups or clubs focused on personal development can also be a great resource. Being part of a community with similar goals and challenges can provide a sense of belonging and a collective energy that uplifts all members.

The Role of Celebration in Stress Management

Understanding Stress Management

Stress management is the process of identifying stressors in one's life and finding ways to reduce or cope with them. It is an important aspect of maintaining mental and emotional well-being, especially for teenagers who are often juggling multiple responsibilities and pressures.

Celebration and Stress Management

Celebration can play a key role in stress management. Taking the time to celebrate achievements can provide a much-needed break from the constant pressure to perform. It allows for a moment of relaxation and joy that can reduce stress levels and rejuvenate the mind and body.

Managing Stress through Celebration

Managing stress through celebration involves consciously using celebration as a tool to combat stress. This means planning for celebrations in advance, using them as incentives to complete tasks, and ensuring that they are a regular part of one's routine. By doing so, teenagers can create positive experiences that counterbalance the stress in their lives.

Case Studies on Celebrating Growth and Progress

Real-Life Examples of Celebrating Growth and Progress

There are many real-life examples of individuals who have effectively celebrated their growth and progress. These stories can serve as inspiration and provide practical ideas for how to incorporate celebration into one's own journey.

Lessons Learned from Case Studies

From these case studies, several lessons can be learned. One key takeaway is the importance of personalizing the celebration to make it meaningful. Another is the value of sharing one's achievements with others to multiply the joy and spread motivation.

Activities for Celebrating Growth and Progress

Practical Exercises for Celebrating Growth and Progress

Practical exercises for celebrating growth and progress include creating a vision board of goals and achievements, writing a letter of congratulations to oneself, or setting up a reward system for reaching milestones.

Reflective Activities for Celebrating Growth and Progress

Reflective activities involve looking inward and assessing one's journey. This can be done through meditation, journaling, or discussing one's experiences with a trusted friend or mentor.

Celebration and Self-Confidence

How Celebrating Growth and Progress Builds Self-Confidence

Celebrating growth and progress can significantly boost self-confidence. It provides evidence of one's capabilities and reinforces the belief in oneself. This increased self-confidence then fuels further growth and progress, creating a positive cycle of development.

The Interplay Between Self-Confidence and Celebration

The interplay between self-confidence and celebration is dynamic. As selfconfidence grows, the desire and ability to celebrate achievements also increase. Conversely, regular celebration can enhance self-confidence by constantly affirming one's worth and abilities.

Celebration and Goal Achievement

The Role of Celebration in Achieving Goals

Celebration plays a crucial role in achieving goals. It serves as a milestone that marks progress and provides a sense of completion. Celebrating also helps to break down larger goals into manageable parts, making the journey towards them more enjoyable and less daunting.

Celebrating Growth and Progress for Goal Achievement

To effectively use celebration for goal achievement, it is important to plan celebrations as part of the goal-setting process. This planning includes deciding how to celebrate different types of achievements and ensuring that the celebrations are proportionate to the milestones reached.

Further Reading

If you're interested in learning more about celebrating growth and progress for goal achievement, here are some recommended books and resources that can provide additional insights:

1. "The Power of Small Wins" by Teresa Amabile and Steven Kramer: This book explores the concept of 'small wins' and how celebrating these can lead to significant progress.

2. "The Progress Principle" by Teresa Amabile and Steven Kramer: From the same authors, this book delves deeper into the idea of recognizing and celebrating progress in our daily lives.

3. "Goals!" by Brian Tracy: A comprehensive guide on setting, pursuing, and achieving goals. It also discusses the importance of celebrating milestones along the way.

Remember, the journey to achieving your goals is just as important as the destination. Celebrating your progress not only makes the journey more enjoyable but also motivates you to keep pushing forward.

Conclusion: The Power of Celebrating Growth and Progress

Reflecting on the Journey of Celebrating Growth and
Progress

Reflecting on the journey of celebrating growth and progress allows individuals to see the full scope of their development. It highlights the importance of acknowledging every step of the journey, not just the destination.

Looking Forward: Celebrating Growth and Progress in the Journey to Mastery

Looking forward, celebrating growth and progress will continue to be an integral part of the journey to mastery. It will serve as a reminder of past achievements and a motivator for future endeavors. By embracing celebration, teenagers can enhance their personal mastery and live a more fulfilled life.

20. LOOKING AHEAD: YOUR JOURNEY TO MASTERY

Understanding Mastery

What is Mastery?

Mastery is the process of becoming outstanding or extremely skilled in a particular subject or activity. It involves a deep understanding and proficiency that allows one to perform at a high level consistently. Mastery is not just about acquiring skills; it's about refining them to the point of excellence and beyond. It's a journey that involves dedication, persistence, and continuous improvement.

To achieve mastery, one must go beyond the basics and delve into the nuances of a subject or skill. It requires a commitment to learning and growth, and the willingness to push oneself beyond comfort zones. Mastery is not a destination but a path of ongoing development where the goal is to keep learning and evolving.

The Role of Mastery in Personal Development

In the context of personal development, mastery plays a

crucial role. It is not only about becoming better at a particular skill but also about developing oneself holistically. Mastery can lead to increased self-awareness, self-discipline, and a sense of purpose. It can help individuals understand their strengths and weaknesses and how to leverage them to their advantage.

The pursuit of mastery can also foster resilience and adaptability, as it often involves overcoming obstacles and adapting to new challenges. As teenagers embark on the journey of personal mastery, they learn valuable life lessons that contribute to their overall growth and maturity.

The Journey to Mastery

Stages of the Journey to Mastery

The journey to mastery can be broken down into several stages. Initially, there is the awareness stage, where one becomes conscious of their interest or passion in a particular area. Following this is the learning stage, where one acquires the basic knowledge and skills necessary to progress.

As one continues, they enter the practice stage, dedicating time and effort to refine their skills. This stage is characterized by repetition and often includes making and learning from mistakes. The next stage is proficiency, where skills become more consistent, and one starts to see significant progress.

The final stage is mastery itself, where one achieves a high level of skill and understanding. However, true mastery is about continual growth, so even at this stage, the journey does not end. Instead, it evolves into a lifelong commitment to excellence and learning.

Understanding the Process of Mastery

Understanding the process of mastery is essential for anyone embarking on this journey. It requires recognizing that mastery is not linear but often involves setbacks and plateaus. It's important to appreciate the value of the process itself and not just the end result.

Mastery is also personal and subjective. What constitutes mastery in one field may differ greatly from another, and what one individual considers mastery may differ from another's view. The key is to define what mastery means to you and pursue it with intention and focus.

Setting Goals for Mastery

Identifying Mastery Goals

Identifying goals for mastery begins with self-reflection. Consider what you are passionate about and where you would like to excel. Goals should be specific, measurable, achievable, relevant, and time-bound (SMART). They should challenge you but also be within reach given your current skills and resources.

When setting goals, think about both short-term objectives that will move you closer to mastery and long-term aspirations that represent the ultimate level of skill you wish to achieve. These goals will serve as a roadmap for your journey.

Creating a Plan for Mastery

Once you have identified your goals, the next step is to create a plan to achieve them. This plan should outline the steps you need to take, the resources you will require, and the timeline you expect to follow. It should also include strategies for overcoming potential obstacles and methods for tracking your progress.

Your plan should be flexible enough to accommodate changes and adaptable to new information or skills you acquire along the way.
Remember, the plan is a guide, not a rigid set of rules.

Maintaining Motivation for Mastery

Maintaining motivation is critical on the journey to mastery. Motivation can come from a variety of sources, such as a desire for self-improvement, the enjoyment of the skill, or the pursuit of a specific goal. It's important to understand what drives you and to remind yourself of these reasons when facing challenges.

Setting and celebrating small milestones can help maintain motivation, as can surrounding yourself with supportive peers and mentors. Additionally, keeping a journal or log of your progress can provide a tangible reminder of how far you've come and inspire you to continue.

Overcoming Challenges in the Journey to Mastery

Identifying Challenges

Challenges are an inevitable part of the journey to mastery. They can take many forms, such as lack of resources, time constraints, or personal doubts. Identifying these challenges early on can help you prepare for them and develop strategies to overcome them.

It's also important to recognize that some challenges may be internal, such as fear of failure or perfectionism. Being aware of these mental and emotional barriers is the first step to addressing them.

Strategies for Overcoming Challenges

Overcoming challenges requires a combination of resilience, problem-solving, and support. Strategies might include breaking down large goals into smaller, more manageable tasks, seeking out additional resources or training, and finding ways to stay inspired and engaged with your skill.

It's also helpful to learn from others who have faced similar challenges. Reading about or talking to those who have achieved mastery can provide valuable insights and encouragement.

Seeking Support for Challenges

No one achieves mastery alone. Seeking support from friends, family, mentors, or a community of like-minded individuals can make a significant difference in overcoming challenges. These supporters can offer advice, encouragement, and sometimes a different perspective that can help you move past obstacles.

Don't hesitate to reach out for help when you need it. Remember that asking for assistance is not a sign of weakness but a strategic move towards achieving your goals.

The Role of a Support System in the Journey to Mastery

Understanding the Importance of a Support System

A support system is a network of people who provide emotional, informational, and practical help. In the journey to mastery, a support system is invaluable. It can provide motivation, feedback, and a sense of accountability. A strong support system can also help you navigate the ups and downs of the journey, keeping you focused and on track.

Your support system can include family, friends, teachers, coaches, or anyone else who is invested in your success and well-being. These individuals can offer different types of support, from a listening ear to specific advice on improving your skills.

Building and Maintaining a Support System

Building a support system involves reaching out to potential supporters and nurturing those relationships. It's important to be clear about the kind of support you need and to be open to receiving it. Regular communication and mutual respect are key to maintaining a strong support system.

Remember to give back to your support system as well. Supporting others in their journey can strengthen your relationships and provide you with additional insights into your own path to mastery.

Leveraging a Support System for Mastery

Leveraging your support system effectively means actively engaging with your supporters. Share your goals, celebrate your successes with them, and seek their input when facing challenges. They can offer different perspectives and solutions that you might not have considered.

Additionally, your support system can hold you accountable to your goals. Knowing that others are aware of your objectives and are cheering you on can be a powerful motivator to stay committed to your journey to mastery.

Biographical Snapshot

Thomas Edison: A Master of Invention

Thomas Alva Edison, one of the world's most famous inventors, is a perfect example of someone who leveraged his support system to achieve mastery. Born in 1847, Edison is credited with developing many devices in fields such as electric power generation, mass communication, sound recording, and motion pictures.

Edison's Support System

Edison's mother, a former schoolteacher, played a significant role in his early education and nurtured his curiosity. His supportive family environment allowed him to explore and experiment from a young age. Later in life, Edison surrounded himself with a team of skilled researchers and workers at his invention factory in Menlo Park. These individuals provided the support, feedback, and diverse perspectives that Edison needed to refine his inventions and bring them to the world.

Accountability and Persistence

Edison's support system also held him accountable. He was known for his tireless work ethic and his famous quote, "Genius is one percent inspiration and ninety-nine percent perspiration." This mindset, coupled with the accountability provided by his team, kept Edison motivated and committed to his journey to mastery.

Edison's Legacy

Edison's mastery in invention has left a lasting impact on the world. His inventions, such as the practical electric light bulb and the phonograph, have shaped modern life as we know it. His story serves as a powerful reminder of the role a support system plays in the journey to mastery.

Case Studies on the Journey to Mastery

Real-Life Examples of the Journey to Mastery

There are countless examples of individuals who have achieved mastery in various fields. Consider the story of a young musician who practiced diligently every day, sought feedback from experienced mentors, and overcame performance anxiety to become a renowned concert pianist. Or the tale of a teenage coder who, through trial and error, self-study, and participation in coding communities, developed an app that solved a common problem and gained widespread acclaim.

These stories illustrate the common themes in the journey to mastery: dedication, persistence, and the willingness to learn from both successes and failures.

Lessons Learned from Case Studies

From these case studies, we can learn that mastery requires time and cannot be rushed. We also see the importance of embracing challenges as opportunities for growth. Moreover, these stories highlight the significance of a support system in providing guidance and encouragement.

Another key lesson is the value of sharing one's knowledge and experiences with others. Many who have achieved mastery find fulfillment in mentoring those who are earlier in their journey, creating a cycle of learning and support.

Think & Reflect

Reflect on Your Journey: Consider your own journey towards mastery. What are some challenges you have faced? How have you turned these challenges into opportunities for growth?

Identify Your Support System: Who are the people in your life that provide guidance and encouragement? How have they helped you in your journey towards mastery?

1. Share Your Knowledge: Think about a time when you shared your knowledge or experiences with someone else. How did it feel?
   Did you learn anything new from the experience?

2. Find a Mentor: Is there someone you admire for their mastery in a certain area? Consider reaching out to them for guidance.

Remember, everyone starts somewhere!
Plan for the Future: What are some steps you can take now to continue on your journey towards mastery? Remember, the journey to mastery is not a sprint, but a marathon. Every step you take is progress.

Activities for the Journey to Mastery

Practical Exercises for the Journey to Mastery

Practical exercises can help solidify the skills needed for mastery. For example, deliberate practice, where you focus on specific aspects of a skill and receive immediate feedback, can lead to significant improvements. Other exercises might include simulation of real-world scenarios, collaborative projects, or competitions that challenge you to apply your skills in new ways.

It's also beneficial to engage in cross-training, where you develop related skills that can enhance your primary area of focus. This can lead to a more well-rounded skill set and prevent burnout by varying your activities.

Reflective Activities for the Journey to Mastery

Reflective activities are equally important in the journey to mastery. Keeping a journal where you reflect on your experiences, challenges, and what you've learned can provide insights into your progress and areas for improvement. Setting aside time for meditation or mindfulness can also help you stay centered and focused on your goals.

Engaging in regular self-assessment, perhaps with the help of a mentor or coach, can help you evaluate your progress and adjust your strategies as needed. Reflection is a powerful tool for personal growth and mastery.

> Mindfulness is a form of meditation where you focus on being intensely aware of what you're sensing and feeling in the moment, without interpretation or judgment. Practicing mindfulness involves breathing methods, guided imagery, and other practices to relax the body and

mind and help reduce stress.

1. Reduced Stress: Mindfulness can help reduce stress and anxiety.

2. Improved Focus: Practicing mindfulness can improve your focus and concentration.

3. Better Emotional Health: Regular mindfulness practice can lead to improved emotional health.

Mastery and Self-Confidence

How Mastery Builds Self-Confidence

As you progress in your journey to mastery, you'll likely notice an increase in self-confidence. This comes from the competence you develop and the successes you experience along the way. Each milestone reached and each challenge overcome contributes to a stronger belief in your abilities.

Self-confidence also grows from the knowledge that you have dedicated yourself to a goal and are making tangible progress. It's the result of knowing that you have the skills and resources to handle whatever comes your way.

The Interplay Between Self-Confidence and Mastery

There is a dynamic interplay between self-confidence and mastery. Confidence can fuel your pursuit of mastery, as it encourages you to take on new challenges and persist in the face of setbacks. Conversely, the process of working towards mastery can bolster your self-confidence.

This positive feedback loop can lead to a virtuous cycle where increased confidence leads to greater mastery, which in turn leads to even more confidence. It's important to nurture both as you progress on your journey.

Mastery and Goal Achievement

The Role of Mastery in Achieving Goals

Mastery plays a significant role in achieving goals, as it equips you with the skills and mindset necessary to reach them. When you are on the path to mastery, you are more likely to set challenging yet achievable goals and to develop the persistence and strategies needed to attain them.

Mastery also involves learning to set goals that are aligned with your values and passions, which can lead to a more fulfilling and motivated pursuit of those goals.

Leveraging Mastery for Goal Achievement

To leverage mastery for goal achievement, it's important to apply the skills and knowledge you've gained in a focused and strategic manner. This might involve breaking down larger goals into smaller, skill-related tasks that you can master one at a time.

It's also helpful to use the principles of mastery, such as deliberate practice and continuous learning, to refine your approach to goal setting and achievement. By doing so, you can increase your chances of success and the satisfaction that comes with it.

The Power of Mastery

Reflecting on the Journey to Mastery

As you reflect on your journey to mastery, consider the growth you've experienced, the challenges you've overcome, and the knowledge you've gained. This reflection is not only about acknowledging your achievements but also about understanding the deeper changes that have occurred within you because of your pursuit of mastery.

Recognize that the journey to mastery is as much about personal development as it is about skill development. The lessons learned, the character built, and the confidence gained are all part of the powerful transformation that mastery can bring.

Looking Forward: Continuing Your Journey to Mastery

Looking forward, your journey to mastery does not end with the achievement of a specific goal. Instead, it's a lifelong process of learning, growing, and refining your skills. Embrace the mindset of a lifelong learner and be open to the endless possibilities that mastery can bring to your life.

As you continue your path, remember to share your knowledge and experiences with others, contribute to your community, and help others on their journey to mastery. In doing so, you not only enrich your own life but also the lives of those around you.

Keep up the good work.

Made in the USA
Columbia, SC
26 January 2025